REVERSE

OBVERSE

The first design of the Seal of the United States, recommended by Franklin, Adams, and Jefferson, the Committee appointed immediately after the Declaration of Independence had been read, July 4, 1776.
[From a drawing by Benj. J. Lossing from the description.]
(*See p. 106-107*)

THE ORIGIN OF REPUBLICAN FORM OF GOVERNMENT
IN THE
UNITED STATES OF AMERICA

BY

OSCAR S. STRAUS, Litt. D., LL. D.

WITH AN INTRODUCTORY ESSAY

BY

M. EMILE DE LAVELEYE

[TRANSLATED FROM THE FRENCH EDITION]

Liberty's Lamp Books
QUINCY, MA

Copyright © 2025 by Liberty's Lamp Books

Original Copyright by G.P. PUTNAM'S SONS, 1885, 1901, 1926

Printed in the United States of America

Cover Design by Sparrow Publishing House & Graphic Design

Liberty's Lamp Books
12 Keyes Street
Quincy, MA 02169
www.libertyslampbooks.com

Book Layout ©2013 BookDesignTemplates.com

Library of Congress Cataloging-in-Publication Data

ISBN 978-0-5784979-3-8

The Origin of Republican Form of Government in the United States of America / by Oscar S. Straus

Contents

Preface

De Laveleye's Introductory Essay

I. Introductory. The American Colonies Prior to the Revolution

II. The Political Causes of the Revolution

III. Religious Causes of the Revolution

IV. The Genesis of the Republic

V. Monarchy and the Church

VI. The Hebrew Commonwealth, the First Federal Republic

VII. The Influence of the Hebrew Commonwealth Upon the Origin of Republican Government in the United States

Notes

Index

DEDICATED

TO THE CHERISHED MEMORY OF

MY MOTHER

The name of Republic will be exalted, until every neighbor, yielding to irresistible attraction, seeks new life in becoming part of the great whole; and the national example will be more puissant than army and navy for the conquest of the world.

—— CHARLES SUMNER'S "Prophetic Voices Concerning America."

PREFACE.

The reasons why the people in the thirteen American colonies, when they dissolved their connection with Great Britain, adopted as their form of polity a Democratic Republic, are usually taken for granted and accepted as a matter of course. I have nowhere been able to find more than a passing allusion to this important subject. During the winter of 1883-4, I delivered two lectures, one in the city of New York and the other before the Long Island Historical Society in the city of Brooklyn. The interest awakened by these lectures induced me to further investigate the subject and embody the result in a more permanent form. That this little treatise is exhaustive of the subject is not claimed, but some facts are presented which I trust may be deemed worthy of consideration. The older and more permanent our government becomes, the greater will be the interest that attaches to its origin and development. Historians have traced the various stages of this development, but I am not aware that it has ever been attempted to present the reasons why the Republican form of government was selected in preference to every other form of polity. I have been led to ascribe its origin mainly to ecclesiastical causes, which operated from the time the Pilgrims set foot upon our continent, and to the direct and indirect influence of the Hebrew Commonwealth. Through the windows of the Puritan churches of New England the new West looked back to the old East.

INTRODUCTORY ESSAY.

By M. Emile De Laveleye

[Translated from the French edition]

In studying the science of institutions and governments, most writers have failed to recognize that overwhelming influence exercised by the religious ideas of the people in the shaping and in the practical working of political constitutions. Recently, Count de Franqueville, in a careful work treating upon the subject of government in England, stated that Protestantism had in no way contributed to the development of English liberty.

It was Montesquieu, however, who said, "The Catholic religion is better adapted to a monarchy, Protestantism the better suited to a republic." I do not think this truth has been more clearly demonstrated than by Edgard Quinet in his "Révolution Française." Here the author shows that the prodigious effort made by France to obtain and organize liberty simply ended with the Caesarism of Napoleon. The reason for this was that political reform did not have for its foundation the principle of religious reform.

Today we can demonstrate by evidence what intelligent thinkers only began to discern in the eighteenth century, because the decisive influence which forms of worship had, not only on politics but also on political economy, was not visible then. Today this principle shines forth, throwing increasing light on contemporaneous events. The influence which religion exercises on man is so profound that its constant tendency must be to shape State institutions in forms borrowed from religious organization.

A question so often asked is this: "Why have there been successful revolutions in the Low Countries, in England, in America, while the French Revolution came to naught?" M. Guizot has written a monograph to elucidate this subject which, thoroughly replying to the question, contains the secret which rules our destinies. On my part I do not hesitate in saying this much: It is because in the first of these examples revolutions were carried out in Protestant countries, and on that account were successful. In the other case, it failed because the country was Catholic.

Voltaire, before this, said as much. He asked: "How is it that the governments of France and England are as different as those of Morocco or Venice? Is it not because the English, always wrangling with Rome, finally shook off a hateful yoke, while a lighter-minded people pretended to laugh and dance in their chains?" Voltaire spoke the truth, but did he not excite to laughter and lead in the dance? There was a closer touch between France and England when the French freed themselves from the yoke of the Church.

Wherever the sovereign lays claim to divine right, there liberty cannot be established. The reasons are evident. The power which talks and acts in the name of God is necessarily absolute. Orders from Heaven are not to be discussed. Simple mortals can only bow and obey. I know of no exception to this rule.

Primitive Christianity favored most particularly the establishment of liberal and democratic institutions. Doubtless, on its ascetic side, it detached man from his worldly interests, while it did not lessen his claims as a citizen. But in elevating and purifying morals he became better fitted for self-government and a free existence. During the early centuries in Christian communities there was perfect equality, because all the power was derived from the people, whose decision and opinion controlled the government. There were no purer democratic republics than the primitive Christian communities. Accordingly, when the Presbyterians of the sixteenth century returned to their old Church organization, they could not help but found a State with republican institutions.

The history of the institution of the Church shows a steady progress towards concentration of power. Drawing itself away from that democracy, that equality of early Christianity, the Church has finally in the nineteenth century become the exponent of papal infallibility; a more complete despotism than this it would be difficult to imagine. It was a democratic republic at the start, but at the finish an aristocracy of bishops independent of the Pope. If civil society tends to mold itself within the lines of a religious association, the facts show that it is invariably under the control of a despotic absolutism. It is so understood by the partisans of the Church.

Bossuet, in his "Politique Tirée de l'Écriture Sainte," traces those conditions which must exist in a Catholic country. "God established kings as His ministers, and through them He reigns over the people." "Royal authority is absolute." "The prince need render account to no one for his actions." "Princes must be obeyed as you would obey the dictates of justice." "They are the gods and participate in some way in divine independence." "As for the subjects, who may oppose the violence of a prince, they may only remonstrate in a respectful manner, but without mutiny or murmur."

The logical deduction from all this must be, that in a Catholic country the government is necessarily despotic; first, because such is the manner of the Church; secondly, because kings held, as it was taught, their power direct from God or the Pope, which power could be neither curtailed nor controlled.

Bossuet, in his own singularly pompous and vigorous language, gives the definition of a monarchy formed in accordance with Roman Catholic tradition, just as it shaped itself from the Rome of the Caesars and the popes.

"You must obey the prince, as you would justice itself. Princes are gods and somehow participate in divine independence. As in God is united all perfection, so in the personality of the prince is the concentration of all power. If God were to withdraw His hand, the world would lapse into chaos. Were authority to cease in the kingdom, all would fall into confusion. Bethink you of the king in his closet. From thence speed the orders which govern the magistrates, the officers, the provinces, and the armies. It is the semblance of God, seated on His throne in the heavenly heights, commanding all the forces of nature. The wicked may try to hide their heads, but the light of God follows them everywhere. This is why God gives the prince the power of discovering all secret wiles. His eyes and hands are everywhere. The birds in the sky tell him all that happens. He has received from God a certain circumspection which is akin to a divine penetration. If he discovers an intrigue, his arms are so long that he can seize his enemies. From the most remote regions of the world he can drag them from the bottom of abysses. There is no refuge from such a power."

The Reformation, on the contrary, was a return to primitive Christianity, and above all towards the democracy of the prophets of the Old Testament, which was alive with the breath of liberty and resistance to absolutism. It tended towards the birth of republican and constitutional institutions.

The Protestant acknowledges in his religion but a single authority, that of the Bible. He would not bow before the authority of a man as would the Catholic. He examines, he discusses all questions for himself.

Calvinists, Presbyterians, having reestablished republicanism within the Church, the Protestants in logical sequence brought into their social polity the same principles and habits. The charge brought by Lamennais against the Reformers is perfectly true. He said: "They denied that power was derivable from religious bodies. It followed that they also denied that power was derivable from political bodies. They substituted in both cases such reason and will as man might possess, in opposition to the reason and will of God. Hence, man was independent, and bent on perfect liberty. He was his own master, his own king, his own God."

Luther and Calvin did not advocate resistance to tyranny; they rather condemned it and extolled obedience. Neither did they admit the fullest liberty of conscience. Despite them, however, the principle of political and religious liberty, that of the sovereignty of the people, is the logical outcome of the Reformation. The proof of this was discoverable in the natural fruitage. The writers of the Reformation invariably advocated the rights of the people, and wherever Protestantism triumphed, there free institutions were established. Their enemies were not deceived. They declared it an evil thing, this union of reform and liberty.

"The Reformers," said a Venetian envoy in France during the sixteenth century, "preached that the king has no authority over his subjects. This way of thinking must lead them towards a government something like that existing in Switzerland and to the destruction of monarchical form of government."[1]

Montluc wrote: "The Ministers preach that kings have no other power but that which pleases the people. Others preach that the nobility are no better than they

---

[1] M. Laurent, "La Rèvolution Française," t. I., § 2, ¶3.

are. That is the spirit of this liberal Calvinism which tends towards equality."¹

Tavannes, time and time again, notes the democratic tendency of the Huguenots. "They are republicans within the royal states, having means of their own, with their soldiery, their distinct finances, and bent on establishing a popular and democratic government."²

The great jurist Dumoulin denounced the Protestant pastors before the Parliament. He said: "They have no other desire than to reduce France into a popular state, and to make it a republic like Geneva. They are trying to abolish hereditary rights by placing on an equal footing the lowest-born with the most exalted. They think that all men, as the children of Adam, are equal by divine and natural law."

The thoughts attributed to the Reformers have the same fundamental ideas as those of the Revolution. If France had adopted them in the sixteenth century she would have enjoyed liberty, self-government, and would have kept to them.

In 1622 Gregory XV. wrote to the King of France, begging him to end the quarrel in Geneva, which was then the headquarters of Calvinism and republicanism. In France, after the death of King Henry IV., the Duke de Rohan, who was a Huguenot, wanted to form a republic, declaring that the time for kings had passed away.

The reproach has been cast on the Protestant nobility for seeking to split up France into petty republican states

---

[1] Blaise de Montluc, "Collection de Mèmoires de Petitot."
[2] Tavannes, même collection, t. XXIII., 72.

like Switzerland, and the chief merit of the Ligue — so it was argued — consisted in having maintained French unity. What the Huguenots wanted were, unquestionably, local autonomy, decentralization, and a federal system which would foster communal and provincial liberty. That is what France is endeavoring in vain to establish today. It was the blind passion for unity and uniformity which wrecked the Revolution, and which too often caused France to revert to despotism. Calvin wished that "the ministers of the Sacred Writ should be elected by the consent and with the approbation of the people, and that pastors should preside over the elections." That was the system Calvinists wanted to introduce into France.

"In the year 1620," says Tavannes, "their state was certainly a democratic one, with mayors and ministers holding all authority. They did not belong to the noble class. Had they accomplished their purpose, the condition of France would have become about the same as that of Switzerland, with the abolition of princes and of the gentry."

No sooner had the Reform placed the gospel in the hands of the peasants, than they clamored in the name of Christian liberty for the abolition of serfdom and a recognition of their ancient privileges. Everywhere claims were advanced for natural rights, liberty, tolerance, and the sovereignty of the people. The writings of the period show this condition of thought. There may be cited, among many publications of the time, a celebrated pamphlet written by Languet, "Junii Bruti Celtae vindiciae contra tyrannos, de principe in populum populique in principem legitima potestate." In the dialogue he writes about "the authority of the prince and the liberty of the people."[1]

These ideas, which stand at the base of modern liberty, always found their most eloquent defenders in Protestantism. Jurieu, the minister, stood as their champion against Bossuet in a celebrated debate. Locke was their exponent in a scientific form. Montesquieu, Voltaire, and other political writers of the eighteenth century all borrowed arguments from Locke, and from them was born the French Revolution. But long before that, these ideas had found their application, and with lasting effect, in Protestant States. First it came about in Holland, then in England, and above all in America.

The famous Edict of July 16, 1581, in which the States-General of the Low Countries proclaimed the forfeiture of the King of Spain, is the clearest consecration of the sovereignty of the people. To dethrone a king it was necessary to invoke this principle: "Subjects are not created by God for the prince, so that the prince must be obeyed in all matters and things, according to his pleasure, but rather the prince depends on his subjects, and over these he may not be the prince save to govern them according to right and reason." The edict went on further to say that the people, in order to escape from the tyranny of a despot, were forced to withdraw their obedience. "There remains no other method whereby we may con-

---

[1] "Mèmoires de l'État de France sous Charles IX.," t. III., 57-64. See also "Révolution Française," I., 345.

serve and defend our ancient liberty, our women, children, and our descendants, in whose behalf, in accordance with the laws of nature, we are ready to risk our lives and our means."

In England the Revolution of 1648 was carried out on the same principles. Milton and other republicans of that epoch defended these principles with admirable vigor and spirit.

It has been our custom to honor the famous principles of '89 as born of the French Revolution. This is a decided historical error. In France eloquent discourses have been devoted to this subject. It is only recently that the most sacred of all rights, liberty of conscience, has been respected.[1] Puritans and Quakers, proclaimed and practiced it two hundred years before in America, and it is from there and England that Europe took the idea, towards the close of the eighteenth century.

As early as 1620 the constitution of Virginia established a representative government, trial by jury, and the principle that taxes should be only voted for by those who had to pay them.

A man arose (1633) who claimed not alone tolerance, but complete equality in all worship before the civil law, and on this principle he founded a State. The man was Roger Williams, and his name, barely known in our continent, is worthy of being inscribed among the benefactors of humanity. He it was who first spoke out for liberty of conscience in a world which for four thousand

---

[1] See a very instructive article by Prevost-Paradol, *Revue des Deux Mondes*, 1858.

years had been steeped in the blood of intolerance. Descartes had declared only in favor of free research in philosophy. Roger Williams was the champion of religious liberty as a political right. "Persecution for cause of conscience," he said, "is most evidently and lamentably contrary to the doctrine of Jesus Christ." "He who commands the ship of state can maintain order on board and conduct his vessel into port, even though the entire crew does not attend divine service." "The civil magistrate's power extends only to the bodies and goods and outward estate of men; it cannot intervene in matters of faith, even to stop a church from apostasy and heresy." "The removal of the yoke of soul-oppression will prove an act of mercy and righteousness to the enslaved nations, so it is of binding force to engage the whole and every interest and conscience to preserve the common liberty and peace."

In Bancroft's admirable history you may read how Roger Williams founded the city of Providence in the State of Rhode Island, on principles then unknown in Europe, save perhaps in the Low Countries. In 1641, when the constitution was established, all the citizens were called on to vote. The founders styled themselves a "democracy," and it was one in the fullest sense, just as Rousseau afterwards understood it. The people directly governed themselves. All citizens, without distinction of belief, were equals before the law, and all the laws were confirmed in the popular assemblies. It was the most radical self-government ever known among human societies, and it has lasted for over two centuries without trouble and without revolution.

The Quakers in Pennsylvania and New Jersey founded their States on similar principles. The power dwells with the people. "We put the power in the people." That is the basis of the New Jersey constitution. The principal clauses are as follows: No man, nor assemblage of men, has power over conscience. No one at any time nor under any pretext can be persecuted or harmed in any manner whatever on account of his religious opinions. The General Assembly is to be named by secret ballot. Every man may elect and be elected. Electors give their deputies obligatory instructions. Should a deputy not fulfil his functions he can be prosecuted. Ten commissioners, elected by the Assembly, exercise executive functions. Judges and constables are elected by the people for two years. Judges preside over the jury, but the deciding power is exercised by the twelve citizens composing it. No one can suffer imprisonment for debt. Orphans are cared for at the expense of the State. Instruction is a public service paid for by the State. Almost similar principles were carried out in Pennsylvania and Connecticut.

That man in his own master, that he is free, that no one can claim service of him, or make a demand on him without his own consent, and that government, justice, and all other powers are derived from the people, this, as an assemblage of principles which modern society strives to enforce, is derived from German tradition. The origin of them all is found among the most races before the development of royal powers. These principles, smothered in the Middle Ages by feudalism, and after the fifteenth century by centralization and absolute monarchism, were only kept alive in Switzerland, England, Holland, and in the United States. This breath of democracy was due to the Reformation and to Hebraism, and it was only in the Protestant countries that these were maintained, and gave to the people order and prosperity. If France had not persecuted, slaughtered, exiled, her own offspring who were converts to Protestantism, she would have developed those germs of liberty and of self-government such as have been preserved in provincial States. This as a truth was absolutely established in a book written by M. Gustave Garrison a number of years ago. Recent investigations and current events bring every year additional arguments in support of this.

In the assemblies held at Rochelle, Grenoble, the States-General of Orleans, the spirit of liberty, the true parliamentary spirit, asserted itself as positively as it did in the English Parliament. There may be found uttered in the clear-cut, strong voice of Calvin, those very words which were so telling in the interest of religion and state polity.

"We will know how to defend against the King our cities without a king," said the Huguenots. There can be no question that had they triumphed, the Huguenots would have founded a constitutional monarchy, such as England had, or a federal republic, as existed in the Low Countries. Had the French nobility kept their spirit of independence, that opposition within the law which had been borrowed from Protestantism would have put limits to the royal power, and France would have escaped the oriental despotism of Louis XV. and his successors. These kings demolished the best characteristics of the nobles.

M. Quinet, in his work on the Revolution, pronounces a severe but just judgement on the French nobility of the epoch. "Having sold their religious faith, how could they establish political faith? In the Fronde the nobility lacking ambition showed their spirit for intrigue. Rebelling against Mazarin they prostrated themselves at once when the King appeared. The fraud of their pretensions was evident. They never guided the French towards liberty."

Francis I., when he gave the signal for the prosecution of the Reformers; Henry IV. in abjuring Protestantism, betrayed, as did the nobility, the true interests of France. That saying, "Paris vaut bien une messe," which the majority of French historians regard as indicative of practical sense, is revolting in its cynicism. To sell yourself, to deny your faith for material advantages, is certainly an act which any honest man must scorn.

France suffers today from this spirit as from the dire consequences of St. Bartholomew and the revocation of the Edict of Nantes. Never were there more terrible attacks made on liberty of conscience.

What France is most in need of are men, who, though they may not break with the traditions of the past, must nevertheless accept the new ideas. Republicans are generally hostile or indifferent to all ideas of religion, just as were our ancestors, or the revolutionists of the last century. They are without that foundation on which they can build a solid edifice. Those, again, who defend religious ideas wish to live under the olde régime, and throw obstacles in the way of all reform.

All modern people yearn for the establishment of a representative and constitutional system. This English system, the seeds of which were first grown in the soil of the ancient Germanic constitution which gave life to Protestantism, does not seem capable of being transplanted so as to thrive in a Catholic country.

Mr. Oscar S. Straus, Minister of the United States, gives in a most interesting work the proofs of that great influence which the remembrance of the Old Testament wrought on the liberties of the English colonies in North America, and how it shaped the form of government adopted by them.

At the period of the American Revolution education was limited. There were not many newspapers, and they were rarely issued more than once a week. The number of subscribers was but few. It was the pulpit which took their place. Pastors in their sermons dealt with politics not less than with religion. Sermons were, for the people, the principal sources of general instruction. These pastors in the way of history knew above all that of the Jewish people. It was in the Bible they increasingly sought both inspiration and example. "If the United States has become republican, it is due to the fact," writes Mr. Straus, "that the Hebrew Commonwealth presented to these pastors the model of a Democratic Republic."

Sir Henry Maine, in his "Popular Government," states that the republican form of government was discredited towards the close of the eighteenth century. Notwithstanding the genius of a Cromwell, the English Republic brought about the restoration of the Stuarts. The greater part of the small continental republics were but oligarchies like Venice. The United Provinces of the Low Countries were in rapid decline. This is what Franklin said: "We have examined the different forms of those republics, which, having been originally formed with the seed of their own dissolution, now no longer exist, and we have viewed modern States all round Europe, but find none of their constitutions suitable to our circumstances."[1]

Before the colonists was the primitive constitution of the Hebrews. Algernon Sidney, whose discourses on government were familiar to the founders of the American federation, had eulogized this constitution. "This government is composed of three organisms, besides the magistrates of the several tribes and cities: they had a chief magistrate who was called a judge, and a council composed of seventy chosen men, and the general assembly of the people."

Is this not an illustration of the three organisms of the American Constitution, the President, the Senate, and a popular Chamber? The first question to be answered was this: Had the people a right to rebel against the power of the King of England? The doctrine of divine right and absolute submission was upheld by the Established

---

[1] Bigelow's "Franklin," III., 388.

Church, and it advanced certain passages in St. Paul and the Evangelists recommending obedience to the established powers. But the Puritans fought against this, the teaching of servitude, and invoked the inspired words which resounded with the democracy of the prophets and of Samuel: "Rebellion to tyrants is obedience to God."

Here is an extract from a sermon delivered by a famous preacher, Jonathan Mayhew, in Boston, May 1766. It gives an idea of that language which, spoken in the pulpit, fired the souls of the people in resisting oppression:

"God gave Israel a king in his anger, because they had not sense and virtue enough to like a free commonwealth and to have Himself for their king — where the spirit of the Lord is there is liberty."

A theologian who then enjoyed great renown, Samuel Langdon, President of Harvard College, in a famous sermon delivered before the Massachusetts Congress, May 31, 1775, thus expresses himself:

"The Jewish government, according to the original constitution, which was divinely established, if considered merely in a civil view was a perfect republic, and let those who cry up the divine right of kings consider that the form of government which had a proper claim to a divine establishment was so far from including the idea of a king, that it was a high crime for Israel to ask to be in this respect like other nations, and when they were thus gratified it was rather as a just punishment for their folly."

In another sermon delivered before the Massachusetts congress, Simeon Howard, the pastor, took for this text the words of Exodus xviii., 2: "Thou shalt provide out of all thy people able men, such as fear God, men of truth, hating covetousness, and place such over them to be rulers." "This shows that the Israelites always exercised the right of electing the chiefs of their nation."

The famous Tom Paine, so well known for his enthusiasm for the French Revolution, which he expressed with such eloquence in Paris, wrote in his book on "Common Sense," the one which Washington admired: "That the Almighty hath here entered his protest against monarchical government is true, or the Scriptures are false."

There is a curious fact which shows how thoroughly the men of the American Revolution were inspired by the remembrance of the Old Testament. There was a committee appointed on the very day of the Declaration of Independence, whose duty it was to choose the legend and the design for the seal of the United States. The design was to represent the Egyptians engulfed in the waters of the Red Sea, and Moses guiding the Jews, and commanding the waters to close over Pharaoh. The motto selected was: "Rebellion to tyrants is obedience to God." The committee was composed of Franklin, Adams and Jefferson.

Such are some of the instructive proofs Mr. Straus brings to bear in a thesis, which I think may be considered as fully demonstrated by him.

At the same time it must not be forgotten that in order to establish free societies and self-government, Americans had only to develop those forms of popular government which they derived from their Anglo-Saxon ancestors. These they revived with their essentially democratic characteristics in the new land. The General Assembly of the township is nothing else than the old *tunscip* of the Saxons, where men free and united administered for themselves their general business, in accordance with the formula recorded by Tacitus in his "Germania," "De minoribus principes consultant, de majoribus omnes." This is a point which Professor Edward Freeman has presented in its fullest sense in his work, "An Introduction to the American Constitutional History." The sources of the republican government of the United States are the Bible and the political institutions of the Germans.

To conclude, I do not think I could do better than by reproducing the few words which M. Anatole Leroy-Beaulieu puts in the mouth of an Israelite who is supposedly present at a banquet celebrating the centenary of 1789. This article, written by an eminent Frenchman is purely an imaginative sketch, but it puts in the cleverest way and in striking relief a great truth.

"The whole year 1789 contains the germ of Hebraism. The idea of right and social justice is an Israelitish idea. The advent of justice on this earth has been the dream of our people. To find the first source of man's rights, we must go back farther than the Reform or the Renaissance, farther back even than antiquity or the Gospel, as far back as the Bible, the Thora, and the prophets. Our rabbis, the Isaiahs and Jeremiahs, were the first revolutionists. They announced that the hills should be levelled, the valleys filled up. All modern revolutions have been the echo of that voice which reverberated in Ephraim. We were still herded in the ghetto, on our shoulders was still bound a yellow cord of infamy, when Christianity sought in our sacred writings the startling principles of its revolutions. From our Bible came the Reformation. From it came the inspirations of the poor wretches of the Low Countries. Puritans in England and America appropriated the language of our judges and prophets. To the Bible belongs the success of those revolutions, of those Anglo-Saxons who boast of being your masters. That superiority they owe to a better acquaintance with Israel. The Huguenots and the Bible would have triumphed in France if only the Revolution had burst forth a century earlier, and in that event it would have had a different issue.

"Liberty, equality, and fraternity of man and of the people, find in the Thora their only solid base, the unity of the human race.

"In teaching and all men descended from one Adam and one Eve, the Bible proclaimed that all were free, equal, and brothers. So in the principles of the Revolution our hopes are the same. For this unity, this fraternity, our prophets show us, have been ours in the past, as they must be in the future. They were Israel's ideals. The Revolution with its hopes is in its issue nothing more than the actual testamentary execution of the will of Isaiah. Social renovation, equality of rights, the uplifting of the lowly, the suppression of privileges, of class barriers, the brotherhood of races, everything aimed at or dreamed of by the Revolution, was proclaimed some twenty-five centuries ago by our own true believers. The reconstruction of Jerusalem, the reign of the son of David described in glorious parables, these are what the Revolution aspires to. It is under this mystic form that the regeneration, the pacification of human society, the coming of the age of reason, the development of wealth and comfort, the miracles of industry, of science, the changes in the face of this earth, are presaged."

For my part I am convinced that future events will show more and more all that humanity owed in the past and will owe in the future to the people of Israel, though there be still some misguided persons who are ungrateful, and who would drive them into the ghetto.

CHAPTER I.

INTRODUCTORY

The American Colonies Prior to the Revolution

My purpose in these pages is to trace the *denouement* of the last act of the great drama of Empire, the origin of Republican Form of Government in the United States of America. Revolutions similar in many respects to the American Revolution had, before the latter occurred, taken place in the history of nations. Prior revolutions, however, either terminated in failure, and are designated in history as rebellions, or when successful, had been so only to the extent of overthrowing the then dominant ruler and putting another in his place, who in a short time relapsed into the abuses of his predecessors, or else the change resulted in the formation of another type of government which contained within itself the same or similar elements of tyranny and oppression. In the oft quoted couplet:

> "For forms of government let fools contest,
> What e'er is best administered is best,"

the philosophical poet Pope, who was born in the year of the Revolution of 1688, expressed in proverbial phrase the experiences of the English, who during the preceding generation had witnessed the establishment of no less than four distinct forms of government, which in this short space of time rapidly succeeded one another. First, Absolutism under the guise of limited monarchy during the reign of Charles I., then Parliamentary government under the Long Parliament, then the Commonwealth, then Absolutism again under the last of the Stuarts, and finally Constitutional Monarchy under William and Mary. All of these governments were administered with such a degree of partiality as to amount to persecution. The Anglicans, the Presbyterians, the Catholics, and Puritans were either persecutors or persecuted, as they happened to be the dominant party or the reverse.

The forms of government that existed in the various American colonies were a mixture of the monarchical and republican types — that is to say, they were as nearly republican as it was possible to be and yet be circumscribed by royal charters and under the ultimate control of the King and Parliament of Great Britain. On the other hand they were as nearly monarchical as it was possible to be three thousand miles distant from the seat of authority. The complaints of the people in the colonies were at no time because of the form of their government, or of that of the mother country, but because of the encroachments upon, and utter disregard of, those natural rights, privileges, and immunities to which they deemed themselves entitled, equally with those residing in England.

A brief outline of the colonial governments before the Revolution will give an idea in what respect they were republican and in what monarchical. In the settlement of the various colonies three distinct forms of government were established, arising from the diversity of circumstances under which the respective colonies were settled, as well as from the various objects of the first settlers. These forms were known as the Provincial or Royal, the Proprietary, and the Charter.

At the Revolution the Royal form existed in seven colonies, Virginia, New Hampshire, North Carolina, South Carolina, New York, New Jersey, and Georgia. Under it the King appointed the Governor and Council for the province, the Assembly was elected by the people. The Council formed the upper house, the lower house being the Assembly. The Proprietary existed in three colonies, Maryland, Pennsylvania, and Delaware. It was in most respects similar to the Royal, with this difference mainly, that to the Proprietor, or person to whom the colony was granted, were delegated the powers of the King. The Charter governments were confined to the New England colonies. To these had been granted charters by the King, which gave them in substance the right of local self-government. In them the Governor, Council, and Assembly were originally, as a rule, chosen by the people. Whatever oppressions and encroachments upon their rights the colonists were made to suffer, came through those agencies of their respective forms of government which owed their existence to the King and Parliament. In the Charter forms, where those agencies did not exist, the King claimed ultimately the right, in opposition to the repeated and firm protests of the colonists, to change, alter, and even to abrogate their charters at his pleasure. The New England, or Charter colonies, believing their liberties secure under the express provisions of their charters, naturally felt most aggrieved at the royal encroachments, and it was not singular that in these colonies the earliest and most determined spirit of independence should have been developed.

The colonies were quite contented, so far as their government and connection with the mother country were concerned, until the passage of the Stamp Act. They had no desire for a government totally independent of England. In 1764 Virginia, in its appeal to Parliament and the King, declared that if the people could enjoy "their undoubted rights, their connection with Britain, the seat of liberty, would be their great happiness."

A separation from Great Britain was viewed with alarm and trepidation, and was not only opposed by the Tory party as a whole, but also by many Whigs, who feared it might lead to anarchy and its attendant evils. Many, again, — especially in New York, New Jersey, Pennsylvania, and in the Southern colonies, — were disposed to trust to the natural laps of time to bring about redress of grievances. There was another class, who, while they favored separation from the mother country, were positively opposed to Republicanism.

The Pennsylvania Assembly (Nov. 9, 1775), mainly through the instrumentality of Dickinson, instructed its delegates in Congress to endeavor to restore harmony between Great Britain and her colonies: "We strictly enjoin you," is the language, "that you, in behalf of this colony, dissent from and utterly reject any propositions, should such be made, that may cause or lead to a separation from our mother country, or a change of the form of this government."[1]

The Assembly of New Jersey, on the 28th of November, directed its delegates "not to give their assent to, but utterly to reject, any propositions, if such should be made, that may separate this colony from the mother country, or change the form of government thereof." Governor Franklin of New Jersey, in his speech to the Assembly, November 16, 1775, said: "As sentiments of independency are by some men of present consequence openly avowed, and essays are already appearing in the public papers to ridicule the people's fears of that horrid measure, and remove their aversions to republican government, it is high time every man should know what he has to expect." The Assembly, in reply, stated that it was aware of such sentiments, and that it had already ex-

---

[1] Reed's "Life of Reed," I., 155. Frothingham's "Rise of the Republic," p. 465.

pressed its detestation of such opinions.[1] The Maryland Assembly (which assembled) on the 7th of December, expressed similar views. The New York Provincial Congress, on the 14th of December, declared that, in their opinion, "none of the people of this colony had withdrawn their allegiance," and that their turbulent state did not arise "from any desire to become independent of the British Crown but solely from the inroads made on both by the oppressive Acts of the British Parliament," devised for enslaving the American colonies.[2] The Delaware Assembly instructed its delegates to promote reconciliation.

By these and similar expressions, and by all the proceedings of the first Congress of delegates that met on the 5th of September, 1774, at Carpenter's Hall in Philadelphia, it distinctly appears that the object sought to be attained was a redress of grievances and not the establishment of a separate and independent government. This Congress in its address to the people of Great Britain directly denies any such purpose. It said: "You have been told that we are impatient of government and desirous of independence. These are calumnies. Permit us to be free of yourselves, and we shall ever esteem a union with you to be our greatest glory and our greatest happiness." And again, in the petition to the King written by Dickinson, containing the ultimate decision of America, the Congress says: "Your royal authority over us and our connection with Great Britain we shall always support

---

[1] *Pennsylvania Evening Post*, Nov. 18, 1775. Frothingham's "Rise of the Republic," p. 466, etc.

[2] *New York Constitutional Gazette*, Dec. 16. 1775.

and maintain." And they besought the King "As the loving father of his whole people, his interposition for their relief, and a gracious answer to their petition." "We ask," they continued, "but for peace, liberty, and safety. We wish not a diminution of the prerogative, nor the grant of any new right."

By the resolution of the Congress on the 10th of May, 1776, it was resolved "to recommend to the respective assemblies and conventions of the United Colonies, where no government sufficient to the exigencies of their affairs had been established, to adopt such a government as should in the opinion of the representatives of the people, best conduce to the happiness and safety of their constituents in particular, and of America in general."[1] President Adams, than whom no one more clearly understood the temper of the American people, nor could better read the signs of the times, in his inaugural address delivered 4th of March, 1797, said: "When it was first perceived in early times that no middle course for America remained between unlimited submission to a foreign legislature and to total independence of its claims, men of reflection were less apprehensive of the danger from the formidable power of fleets and armies

---

[1] Elliot's Debates, vol. I., 54. "The Declaration we commemorate expressly admitted and asserted that 'Governments long established should not be changed for light and transient causes.' It dictated no special forms of government for other people and hardly for ourselves. It had no denunciations or even disparagements for monarchies or for empires, but eagerly contemplated, as we do at this hour, alliance and friendly relations with both." — Hon. Robt. C. Winthrop, Centennial Oration, Boston, July 4, 1876.

they must determine to resist, than from those contests and dissentions which would certainly arise concerning the forms of government to be instituted over the whole and over parts of this extensive country."

The Declaration of Independence was no formative act. It asserted liberty, but did not organize it; it was what its title implies, a solemn statement of the grievances of the oppressed and outraged colonists against the tyranny of their rulers, setting forth plainly, vigorously, and eloquently the reasons for their action, grounded upon "self-evident truths," upon those fundamental rights of man and principles of civil liberty which were as old as the Bible, and had been asserted again and again under various forms and not unlike circumstances by every uprising of the people against the injustice and oppressions of the governing power, which had taken place from the days of Moses until the Declaration was published to the world. As to the objects of the Declaration, let the author speak for himself: it was "not to find out new principles or new arguments never before thought of, not merely to say things which had never been said before, but to place before mankind the common-sense of the subject, in terms so plain and firm as to command their assent and to justify ourselves in the independent stand we are compelled to take."[1] It was not a dissertation on government, nor concerning the forms of government, nor did it propose any other change than the transformation of the colonies into "free and independent States." While it provided for a *new* State, it did not contemplate a *new*

---

[1] Letter by Jefferson to Henry Lee, May 8, 1825.

species of State. It nowhere even so much as hinted at a preference for one species of government over another — that was not in the contemplation of the instrument. "We hold these truths to be self-evident," is the language: "that all men are created equal; that they are endowed by their Creator with certain inalienable rights; that among these are life, liberty, and the pursuit of happiness; that to secure these rights, governments are instituted among men, deriving their just powers from the consent of the governed; that, whenever any form of government becomes destructive of these ends, it is the right of the people to alter or to abolish it, and to institute a new government, laying its foundation on such principles and organizing its powers in such form as to them shall seem most likely to effect their safety and happiness."

The closing scene of the great drama of Empire was being enacted, this solemn protest of the American people against every form of arbitrary power. The manifestations of the same forces that brought about the Revolution of 1688 also produced the Revolution of 1776; with this difference, that the English revolution stopped when the constitutional limitations had been placed around the prerogatives of the crown, while the American revolution was a grand step onward, destined to transfer the sovereign powers of the crown to the people, to whom they always belonged, but with whom they so rarely abided.[1] The might, the right, and the power, of the people having been wrested from them in

---

[1] "The Development of Constitutional Liberty in the English Colonies of America," by E.G. Scott (1882), pp. 15-19.

the dawn of history and exalted so high over their heads by the arts of designing princes, that they prostrated themselves before this trinity of their own creation and worshipped it under the form of "Divine right of kings." The usurper's title, through ages of wrongs and bloody oppressions, by the servility of cunning ecclesiastics, went through an evolution of fanatical consecration, and thereby transformed its bearer into a demi-god under the appellation of "King by the Grace of God." The natural notions of polity, by violent restraints put upon the promulgating of any juster derivation of the rights of mankind, were erased out of the minds of men, and they were imbued with a confused notion of something adorable in monarchs as the personal representations of the Divinity. So habituated were the people to the pomp and the power of monarchy, that they blindly and by force of habit associated with it their most exalted ideas of natural right and personal liberty. The claims of the British monarch to these divine attributes had not been abandoned, as we shall have occasion to show in another chapter, so far as the colonies were concerned, at the time even immediately prior to our revolution.

The Declaration of Independence was so radical a protest against this absurd worshipping of kingly person and power, that some of the churches of the colonies had to change their litany to conform with its teachings.[1] In

---

[1] "This day (29th July, 1776), the Virginia convention resolved that the following sentences in the morning and evening church service shall be omitted: 'O Lord, save the King and mercifully hear us when we call upon thee.' That the fifteenth, sixteenth, seventeenth, and eighteenth sentences in the Litany for the King's majesty and the Royal family, etc., shall be omitted.

our day we can with difficulty form a correct conception of what mighty battles of reason had to be fought in order to educate the popular mind up to the standard which made the Declaration of Independence possible; and after the Declaration, all through the trying period of the revolution, what a moral force and power of persuasive argument it required, especially during intervals of reverses, to keep alive the spirit of liberty; or even after the revolution, until the adoption of the Constitution, what a power of lofty patriotism based upon the fundamental principles of natural right was brought into living action to overcome the hereditary awe for royalty and the confused notions as to "unlimited submission." Such revolutions as that of 1776 had taken place before. They had occurred in Greece, in Rome, in Carthage, in Switzerland, in Holland, and even in England. What distinguishes the Revolution of 1776, and marks it with such singular pre-eminence, is not its feats of bravery, though they were by no means insignificant; not its duration, for it was short compared with many wars that history records; not the numbers that were brought face to face in hostile array, for the armies were but insignificant compared with those that had contended on many blood-dyed battlefields; but the results that followed, — the glorious fact that the crown was lifted from the royal

---

That the two prayers for the King's majesty and the Royal family in the morning and evening service shall be omitted. That the prayers in the Communion service which acknowledge the authority of the King, and so much of the prayer for the church militant as declares the same authority, shall be omitted." — *New York Gazette*, July 29, 1776.

brow and placed upon the head of the people, that civil liberty gained all the sword had won.

The ever-important questions of political development are: By what means were these results attained? From what sources of political science did the great founders of our government draw their inspiration? What guiding precedents sanctified by authority did they follow? What models applicable by reason of the blessings of liberty thereunder secured did they adopt? It is an established fact in the history of nations, that systems are reformed by reverting to first principles. The accumulated rubbish of ages is dug away and the pillars of state are made to rest on original and firm foundations. Says Dr. Price, the philosophical author and distinguished contemporaneous observer of early American political affairs: "The colonies were at the beginning of this reign (Geoge III.) in the habit of acknowledging our authority, and of allowing us as much power over them as our interest required; and more, in some instances, than we could reasonably claim. By exertions of authority which have alarmed them, they have been put upon examining into the grounds of all our clams. Mankind are naturally disposed to continue in subjection to that mode of government, be it what it will, under which they have been born and educated. Nothing rouses them into resistance but gross abuses or some particular oppressions out of the road to which they have been used."[1]

When England began her encroachments upon the rights and liberties of the colonies, their first step was to

---

[1] "Observations on the Nature of Civil Liberty," etc., p. 34.

petition for relief, the next was recourse to reason and argument and appeals to the principles of right and justice, and their natural ultimatum was the implements and munitions of war to defend their lives, protect their liberty, and preserve their property. While it is true that the Revolution of 1688 had secured for England definite constitutional rights, the effect was not the same in the colonies. If the rights the colonies then were permitted to enjoy can be termed liberty, it was only that unsettled and restricted kind of liberty that the English people possessed before the Bill of Rights. Even William III., who was born a citizen of a republic, a descendent of the founders of Batavian liberty, who might naturally have been expected to be a friend of popular institutions, was no herald of liberty to the colonies. His course was as absolute towards them as that of the Stuarts. He revived against them the navigation acts, and also the Board of Trade and Plantations. He withheld from them the writ of *habeas corpus*, and he and his successor violated, changed, and abrogated their charters. What was acknowledged as the constitutional rights of the Englishman was denied to the Americans. This was forcibly set forth in the address of the delegates in Congress to the people of Great Britain, bearing the date 5th of September, 1774, in the following language: "Can the intervention of the sea that divides us cause disparity in rights, or can any reason be given why English subjects who live three thousand miles from the royal palace should enjoy less liberty than those who are three hundred distant from it?" The consequence was that the people in America had to fight over again the same battles for constitutional liberties which the English had fought before them, and in fighting them they were brought face to face with natural rights, the basis of all sovereignty and government. George III., so far as his claims over the colonies were concerned, relied as much upon the kingly prerogatives, the doctrine of "Divine Right," as ever did James I. All of these pretensions, all of the questions of right and liberty, had to be argued. To refute this false theory of kingly power it was not only expedient but necessary to revert to the earliest times, to the most sacred records, the Old Testament, for illustrations and for argument, chiefly because the doctrine of "Divine Right," "King by the Grace of God," and its corollaries, "unlimited submission and non-resistance," were deduced, or rather distorted from the *New Testament*,[1] having been brought into the field of politics with the object of enslaving the masses through their religious creed. This incubus had to be lifted from the science of politics before the simplest principles of personal liberty could logically be contended for. It was of first importance to employ such argument as possessed the sacred stamp of the Scriptures. Any other, though as conclusive as mathematical axiom, would not avail, especially among those to whom the Bible was a political as well as a religious textbook and of infallible authority. These authorities and arguments were found in the Old Testament, woven into the history and development of the Hebrew Com-

---

[1] Romans xiii., 1-8. I. Peter ii., 13 and 14.

monwealth.¹ In what manner and with what force and effect they were employed will be seen in the succeeding chapters.

---

¹ "It is, at least, an historical fact, that in the great majority of instances the early Protestant defenders of civil liberty derived their political principles chiefly from the Old Testament, and the defenders of despotism from the New. The rebellions that were so frequent in Jewish history formed the favorite topic of the one — the unreserved submission inculcated by St. Paul, of the other. When, therefore, all the principles of right and wrong were derived from theology, and when by the rejection of traditions and ecclesiastical authority, Scripture became the sole arbiter of theological difficulties, it was a matter of manifest importance, in ascertaining the political tendencies of any sect, to discover which Testament was most congenial to the tone and complexion of its theology." — Lecky's "Rationalism in Europe," vol. II., 168.

CHAPTER II.

The Political Causes of the Revolution

The impelling causes of the revolution were of two separate and distinct classes, which became united during the decade immediately preceding that event. They were religious and political, or the long and the short causes respectively. In this chapter we shall confine ourselves to summarizing the political causes, even at the risk of repeating that which is familiar to the general reader, so that they may be more readily contrasted with the religious causes, which will be considered in the succeeding chapters.

In the American colonies both the desire and purpose of establishing a separate, independent or republican form of government were of very slow growth.[1] Not one

---

[1] The *New York Gazette* of April 8, 1776, contains a paper entitled "Plan of the American Compact." The writer asks: "For what are we to encounter the horrors of war?" etc. He answers: "It is a form of government which Baron Montesquieu and the best writers on the subject have shown to be

of the statesmen who assisted in the framing of the new government had been originally a republican. Even Jefferson, as late as August, 1775, in a letter to John Randolph, expresses himself as belonging to that class of Americans who had rather be dependent upon England, under proper limitations, than to be dependent on any other nation or on no nation whatsoever. The people who planted the colonies were originally subjects of rival powers, and this circumstance was an additional incentive for their successors to cherish their allegiance to England, with the object of claiming the protection of the mother country against the threatening aggressions of other European nations, as well as against the encroachments of one colony upon the other. The Congress that adopted the Declaration of Independence recognized the natural tendency of every people to hold fast to the blessings of peace rather than to resort to the arbitrament of war so long as "ills are sufferable." Its words are: "Prudence indeed will dictate that governments long established should not be changed for light and transient causes; and accordingly all experience hath shown that mankind are more disposed to suffer while ills are sufferable, than to right themselves by abolishing the forms to which they are accustomed. But when a long train of abuses and usurpations, pursuing invariably the same

---

attended with many mischiefs and imperfections, while they pay high encomiums on the excellency of the British Constitution. The Continental Congress has never lisped the least desire for independency or republicanism. All their publications breathe another spirit." This plan was reprinted in pamphlet, entitled "Observations on the Reconciliation of Great Britain and the Colonies."

object, evinces a design to reduce them to absolute despotism, it is their right, it is their duty to throw off such governments, and to provide new guards for their future security. Such has been the patient sufferance of these colonies; and such is now the necessity which constrains them to alter their former systems of government."

In the struggle between England and France for dominion in America, not one of the colonies proved false to its allegiance. Their zeal surpassed even that of the mother country. The war was not undertaken for the relief or the advantage of the colonies, but to gratify the ambition of England by enlarging its colonial dominion, yet as they had derived from its successful ending considerable benefit, this fact was made the plausible basis for the claim that they ought to bear a portion of the burden of expense it had entailed upon the nation. The fact that the colonies had of their own accord already contributed about twenty-five thousand lives and over sixteen millions of dollars, was not considered, or if taken into account did not serve to restrain the rapacity of George III., his ministers and Parliament. Whatever serious differences, if any there were, between the colonies and the mother country, prior to this war, had been removed by its successful termination. "This event," says Pitkin, "produced great joy amongst the colonists, and was accompanied with feelings of gratitude toward the young prince (Geoge III.), in whose reign it was accomplished. Their feelings would have continued but for new encroachments upon their rights."[1] These encroachments were not slow in coming.

England no longer requiring the aid of the colonies upon the continent of America, through whose arms and money she had vanquished her most powerful rival, sought to make them contribute to lighten the pressure of the general expense of the home government. In accordance with this policy, Parliament attempted to put into execution an act passed many years before under George II., but which had become a dead letter upon the statute books, "An act for the better securing and encouraging the trade of his Majesty's colonies in America," commonly known as the "Molasses Act," whereby a duty of six pence was placed on molasses and other articles, being in some instances on half of their value.

A determined attempt to enforce these laws to the letter was the forerunner of a system of direct taxation, the result of which, if allowed to begin, no one could foretell. Cruisers were stationed along the coast, custom-house officers and informers were stimulated by offers of reward, and writs of assistance were granted which gave the possessor the right to search and seize merchandise, on the plea that it was smuggled, no name or specific offense being set out in the writ; the officer holding it could select any house he saw fit and search it, he alone being sole judge if there existed probable cause for so extraordinary a proceeding, which was a gross violation of that sacred principle of the common law, that every man's house is his castle. The legality of these writs was

---

[1] Pitkin's "History of the U.S.," vol. I., 155.

denied. When the cause which was to determine this question came on for trial in the city of Boston, in the council chamber of the Old Town House in February, 1761, James Otis, a lawyer of marked ability, resigned his lucrative office of advocate-general of the Crown, which would have obliged him to argue in favor of the writs, and together with Oxenbridge Thatcher appeared as counsel for the petitioner in opposition thereto. Here was ignited the torch of liberty that kindled the bonfires of the Revolution. "Then and there," according to John Adams, who was present at the hearing, "was the first scene of the first act of opposition to the arbitrary clams of Great Britain. Then and there the child Independence was born. In fifteen years — that is, in 1776, he grew up to manhood and declared himself free." Otis is described upon this argument as being "a flame of fire." He stood up as the bold and brilliant advocate of colonial rights and human liberty. It was he who on this occasion uttered the stirring words, the very keynote of independence, "Taxation without representation is tyranny." The plea of Otis, formulated in legal terms and in eloquent phrases the rights and grievances of the colonies. It asserted principles and cited proof to sustain them, the truth of which was felt before, but never until now so boldly and forcibly expressed. The court has not to this day given its decision; that decision was destined to be written in the blood of revolution, and is now recognized as of binding authority by all constitutional governments of the earth.

The need and greed of England kept the colonies in constant alarm. In February, 1765, Mr. Grenville, the King's Prime-Minister, introduced into Parliament the bill which is known as the Stamp Act, and which passed with but little opposition. The law was not to go into effect until about eight months after its passage. As soon as the news of the passage of this bill reached America, newspapers, pamphlets, and the pulpits issued their protests against it in words so forcible and direct that did not leave men to doubt that the colonies knew their rights, and that unless England would soon retract its policy, they would have the courage to maintain them at the hazard of their lives and fortunes. The General Court of Massachusetts assembled in May, and immediately resolved that all the colonies should be invited to send delegates to a general congress, to be held in New York the October following, to consult together on the present state of affairs, and to determine the course to pursue. An agreement not to import any goods from England till the obnoxious act should be repealed was very generally entered into. Delegates from nine colonies assembled in New York on the 7th of October, they published a Declaration of Rights, and addressed a petition to the King and to the two houses of Parliament. After a session of little more than a fortnight this congress, known as the "Stamp Act Congress," dissolved. The cause of the colonies was taken up in England by some of her ablest statesmen, amongst whom was William Pitt, afterwards Earl of Chatham, energetically seconded by Conway, Colonel Barré, and, also, by Lord Camden, afterwards the Lord Chancellor, one of the highest legal authorities in the realm. This powerful opposition brought about a change of ministry in July, 1765. Dr. Franklin, who lived during this time in London, as the agent of the colony of Pennsylvania, was summoned before the House of Commons, in a committee of the whole, to be examined touching the wishes and feelings of the colonies. The examination lasted ten days.

The Journal of the Commons records: "February 13, 1766, Benjamin Franklin, having passed through his examination, was excepted from further attendance"; and, February 24th, the committee reported "that it was their opinion that the House be moved that leave be given to bring in a bill to repeal the Stamp Act"; and on the 18th of March the repeal was signed. Franklin's testimony served to inform the people of England of the precise attitude of the colonies, as well as the grounds upon which they rested their opposition to such legislation. A brief extract from this examination will give the best insight into the question at issue:

"Q. If the Stamp Act is not repealed, what do you think will be the consequence?

"A. A total loss of the respect and affections the people of American bear to this country, and of all the commerce that depends on that respect and affection.

"Q. If the Stamp Act should be repealed, would it induce the Assemblies of America to acknowledge the right of Parliament to tax them?

"A. No, never! No power, how great soever, can force men to change their opinions."

It had been argued that this class of legislation was just, as a means of compelling the colonies to reimburse England in part for the money spent on their account in wars with the French and the Indians. How this was met and refuted by Franklin this examination will show.

"Q. Do you think it right that America should be protected by this country, and pay no part of the expense?

"A. That is not the case. The colonies raised, clothed, and paid, during the last year, nearly twenty-five thousand men, and spent many millions." He further testified concerning the French and Indian wars: "I know that the last war is commonly spoken of here as entered into for the defense, or for the sake, of the people of America. I think it is quite misunderstood. It began about the limits between Canada and Nova Scotia; about territories to which the Crown indeed laid claim, but which were not claimed by any British colony. None of the lands had been granted to any colonist; we had therefore no particular concern, nor interest in that dispute."[1]

Another equally high authority, one of the greatest philosophers of his time, and no indifferent observer of Britain's treatment of her colonies, Dr. Richard Price, said: "But we have, it is said, protected them and run deeply in debt on their account. Will anyone say that all we have done for them has not been more on our own account, than on theirs? The full answer to this has been already given. Have they made no compensation for the protection they have received? Have they not helped us pay our taxes, to support our poor, and to bear the bur-

---

[1] Hansard, XVI., 205, etc.

den of our debts, by taking from us, at our own price, all the commodities which we can supply them? In short, were an accurate account stated, it is by no means certain which side would appear to be most indebted."[1]

Every new attempt of Parliament to enforce under a different guise its unjust claims of taxation, met with renewed resistance and with stronger opposition, thereby alienating more and more the affection of the colonies, and to that extent tended to unite them in a closer union. The rejoicings caused by the repeal of the Stamp Act had scarcely ceased when another act was passed by Parliament with the same object in view, imposing duties on all teas, paper, glass, paint, and lead, that should be imported into the colonies. This act was passed under the guise of regulating trade, and was intended to escape the objections made against the former act, as the tax was *external*. The flame of the opposition was kindled anew, non-importation agreements were renewed, extending not only to taxed articles, but to all British commodities. This struck straight back into the pocket of the English people, which, to a commercial nation, is always a most sensitive and vulnerable point of attack. The colonists petitioned for the repeal of the act, and in compliance with their demand the duty was taken off from all the articles mentioned save only tea; this was but a paltry tax, being three pence per pound, with a drawback on the value, of a shilling on the pound, the amount originally paid on the importation of the article into Great Britain;

---

[1] "Observation on the Nature of Civil Liberty," etc., by Richard Price (1776), p. 22.

which resulted in making the price of the tea lower than if there were no tax or drawback. The question at stake was not the three pence, but the right of Britain to levy the tax. This once acquiesced in, other taxes would inevitably follow.

The Massachusetts Assembly met and determined on stringent measures. It was resolved to send a petition to the King wherein were set forth the conditions of their settlement as a colony, and maintaining that there could not be taxation without representation; they also protested against the presence of a standing army. Governor Bernard and the Crown officers sent to the King counter-memorials, setting forth the rebellious attitude and independent spirit of the colonists, and recommending the presence of a fleet and troops. In 1768, two regiments of British troops, which were subsequently increased to four, were sent to Boston, which was then, and had always been, the hotbed of opposition. Conflicts between the citizens and the revenue officers in Rhode Island and elsewhere were reported, and the people in Boston became every day more irritated by the presence of soldiers who were there for the purpose of dragooning the people into submission. The General Assembly, foreseeing that a conflict between the citizens and soldiers was likely to occur at the slightest provocation, and desirous of avoiding any hostile collision, requested Governor Hutchinson that the troops be withdrawn. This request was denied, the Governor shielding himself by asserting lack of authority. On the 5th of March, 1770, a conflict between the citizens, or rather a mob, and the soldiers took place, insults were followed by missiles and missiles by fire and shot, then by promiscuous firing from a number of soldiers, whereby three of the citizens were killed and several wounded. This collision was exaggerated until it gained the alarming title of the Boston Massacre. The anniversary of this event, celebrated by public gatherings and by the pulpit, served to inflame the passions of the multitude and to develop and keep alive resistance to English authority. The fact was lost sight of that the officers and soldiers who had fired on the populace, and were indicted and tried for murder, were all acquitted except two, these being found guilty of manslaughter and slightly punished, and that they had been defended by John Adams and Josiah Quincy, two young lawyers who were among the most ardent of the popular leaders.

The "Molasses Act" was one of the first causes of bitterness between England and her colonies; the "Sugar Act" in 1764 did not at all sweeten these relations; and now, in 1773, the kettle of discord was destined to boil by reason of the duty on tea. In this year the contest was brought to a crisis by reason of arrangements which were entered into on the part of the ministry with the East India Company for the consignment of several cargoes of tea to the principal American ports. The tax on tea had been retained for the express purpose of upholding and vindicating the authority of Parliament. This tax was substantially nullified, partly by smuggling, and partly because America did not import much of this commodity. As soon as this project with the East India

Company became known in the colonies, steps were taken to counteract it. At Philadelphia a public meeting was held; eight resolutions were passed against taxation by Parliament, and denounced as an enemy to his country "whoever shall aid or abet in unloading, receiving, or vending the tea." In Boston a town-meeting was held at which Hancock presided, and adopted the Philadelphia resolutions. A committee was appointed to wait upon the consignees and request them to resign the cargoes. This the consignees refused to do. On December 16th the crisis was reached by a band of about fifty men, dressed as Mohawk Indians, boarding the tea vessels and emptying three hundred and forty-two chests in the water. History doth not record who these fifty men were. Circumstances would seem to indicate they were not of that class that constitute mobs, but men who acted no insignificant part in the stirring events that made the next ten years memorable for all time to come. When the news of this occurrence reached England the indignant ministry resolved to mete out punishment to the rebellious Bostonians. An act was passed to shut up the port of Boston, known as the "Boston-Port Bill"; a second, "for better regulating the government of Massachusetts Bay," amounting practically to an abrogation of the charter. A third act, intending not only to meet cases like the Boston Massacre, but reaching much further, provided for the trial in England of all persons charged in the colonies with murder or other capital offenses. A fourth provided for the quartering of troops, four more regiments being sent to Boston, so that the town was now strongly guarded. General Gage, who was directed to resume command, was also commissioned, as Governor of Massachusetts, to succeed Hutchinson. A fifth bill, known as the "Quebec Act," passed at the same session, for the purpose of preventing Canada from joining with the other colonies. It guaranteed to the Catholic Church possession of its vast amount of property and full freedom of worship. The boundaries of the province were also extended to the Mississippi on the west and the Ohio on the south, so as to include, besides the present Canada, the territory of the five States that are now northwest of the Ohio. This last act, with the exception perhaps of the Boston Port Bill, was most effectual in alienating the colonies. It was construed as an effort on the part of Parliament to create an Established Church, and that not alone, but the establishment of *that* church which was most hateful to and dreaded by the great majority of the people in the colonies. The object Parliament intended to effect by the passage of this act was purely one of state policy, and so far as Canada herself was concerned, it was a wise and diplomatic step. But viewed from the side of the other colonies, it had quite a different character. It was regarded as an experiment for setting up an arbitrary government in one colony which was more submissive than the others, in order to extend by degrees a like method of government over all the other colonies. Had an equally conciliatory course been followed by England toward her own original colonies, which were bound to the mother country by all the ties of loyalty, origin, kindred, a common tongue, and the Protestant religion, what happened in respect to Canada would undoubtedly have been the result in the other colonies. Canada had been won by conquest, having been ceded to England only twelve years before this time, by the Peace of Paris, in 1762. Force was the only bond of union between her and England. A breach between England and her other American colonies now existed, which the first four bills above referred to were not likely to mend, but, on the contrary, to widen. Such being the circumstances, Parliament foresaw that Canada would probably embrace this opportunity to rid herself of the power that held her; so it threw to her the bait that she would be most likely to take — the two matters that lay closest to the hearts of the people of that province — the substitution of the French civil or Roman law in all civil matters, and the establishment of the Catholic religion. The ancient hostility between Romanism and Protestantism was thus utilized and placed as a wedge of separation between Canada and the thirteen colonies.[1]

The particulars of the destruction of the tea were received in London by the New York mail on January 19. 1774. On the 7th of March the King in messages to both Houses recommended the matter to their serious consid-

---

[1] This subject was very pointedly referred to by the minority in the House of Commons when the Quebec Act came up for discussion. It was claimed that this measure could not fail to add to the discontent and apprehension of the other colonies, in that they could attribute the extension given to arbitrary military government, and to a people alien in origin, laws, and religion, as the Canadians were, to nothing else but the design of utterly extinguishing the liberties of the other American colonies, and bringing them, by the arms of those very people whom they had helped to conquer, into most abject vassalage. — See Dodsley's *Annual Register* for 1774, p. 76.

eration. The Boston-Port Bill was moved by Lord North on the 14th of March, and on the 31st it received the royal assent and became a law. The act was received in Boston on the 10th of May; it was printed soon after on paper with mourning lines. The Committee of Correspondence invited the committees of eight neighboring towns to meet for deliberation in Faneuil Hall. Samuel Adams presided and Joseph Warren drew up its papers. The inhabitants addressed a circular-letter to all the sister colonies. The effect of the reception of these circulars in the various colonies was the noble purpose to stand by Massachusetts. Providence resolved that all the colonies were concerned in the Port Act, and recommended a congress. In Virginia the House of Burgesses, in resolutions penned by Jefferson, declared that an attack made on one colony was an attack on all, and recommended that the Committee of Correspondence communicate with other committees on the expediency of holding an annual congress. Expressions in favor of a general congress of all the colonies came pouring in from all sides. The people were aroused. The Tories favored the measure as a means most likely to obtain a redress of grievances, and the Whigs as the first move toward resisting the encroachments of Parliament and for bringing the colonies into a firmer union.[1] The *Boston Evening Post* of June 20th stated that a congress "was the general desire of the continent, in order to agree on effectual measures

---

[1] For a very minute summary of the action taken in the various colonies relating to a congress the reader is referred to Richard Frothingham's excellent work, "Thee Rise of the Republic of the U.S.," p. 332, etc.

for defeating the despotic designs of those who were endeavoring to effect the ruin of the colonies."

CHAPTER III.

Religious Causes of the Revolution

The religious element of the revolution was imparted to it by the very circumstances which caused in September, 1620, a company of English Protestants, exiles for religion, to encounter the dangers of the deep and set sail for a new world, and by the causes which impelled Winthrop and his band of Puritans ten years after to fly from the tyranny of Laud, and settle along the northern shores of Massachusetts Bay. "It is certain that civil dominion was but the secondary motive, religious the primary, with our ancestors in coming hither and settling in this land."[1]

A distinction is to be noted between the two colonies above mentioned, in respect to their attitude toward the Established Church. The first of these colonies is known as the Pilgrims, the second as the Puritans. The Pilgrims

---

[1] President Ezra Stiles.

organized as a church before they left Holland; they were independents in religion and were separated entirely from the Church of England. Their residence in Holland had made them acquainted with various forms of religion, and had the effect of emancipating them to a degree from bigotry and intolerance; wherefore they manifested in their subsequent history a much more tolerant and liberal spirit than their brethren of the Bay. They maintained that ecclesiastical censures were wholly spiritual, and not to be visited with temporal penalties. The Puritans of Massachusetts Bay Colony were not separated from the Church of England, "though they scrupled conformity to several of its ceremonies." The reign of James I. was a period of transition from arbitrary government to an incipient assertion of popular rights, and his long and continuous quarrels with Parliament led to an investigation of political principles, and to the questioning of the claims of arbitrary power. The Puritans were at the bottom of this conflict, and during its continuance they grew in numbers, in hope, and in courage. In 1625 James died, and the accession of a new sovereign was an opportune occasion for the friends of popular rights to organize. What was at first a question in the Church concerning ceremonies was now transformed into a principle in politics, between the King on the one side and the Parliament on the other. For four years more under Charles the conflict went on in this form, when a temporary victory was gained for royalty by the King dissolving the third Parliament in a passion, in utter contempt of every claim and principle of popular right.

When the Parliament of 1629 was dissolved all hopes of relief through legislative means had to be abandoned. The powers of Church and State were now allied in an aggressive policy against puritanism and freedom. Laud, the most despotic of bishops, was by Charles promoted step by step in the episcopal office till, in 1633, he was consecrated Archbishop of Canterbury, the primate of the Episcopal Church, the representative man of the Hierarchy, and chief of the High Commission.

"As this dismal state of things approached, and especially when it was reached, patriotic and religious Englishmen asked themselves, and one another what was the course of honor and of safety. While some among them still looked for relief to a renewal and a happy issue of the struggle that had been going on in Parliament, and resigned themselves to await and help on the progress of a political and religious reformation in the kingdom; others, less confident, or less patient, pondered on exile as the best resource, and turned their view to a new home on the Western Continent."[1] The class of emigrants that were now coming to America were of a grade socially and intellectually superior to the Pilgrims. There were among them clergymen and physicians, university graduates, and English country gentlemen of no inconsiderable fortunes. The causes and motives that impelled them to leave homes of ease and comfort in England, and the pleasant society of friends, to risk the dangers of the deep and the still greater dangers and uncertainties that awaited them on land, were not such as would be likely to

---

[1] Palfrey's "History of New England," vol. I., 93.

leave only a fading impression on them or their immediate descendants. The colonists were not adventurers who had all to gain and nothing to lose. They were not men who were driven by a restless spirit of enterprise, or by thirst for gold, but purely by a desire for the enjoyment of spiritual liberty without which life was to them unendurable, and for the love of which they were ready to hazard all. The motives which actuated these early colonists were in one sense narrow and selfish, but of that kind of selfishness which is so near akin to public virtue, that it is frequently confounded with it. Hence arises the abuse and reproach which many writers heap upon our Puritan forefathers for the bigotry and intolerance which characterize their early history, forgetting, or losing sight of the fact that they came here purely and simply to seek freedom of worship for themselves, and that they founded their colonies so that they might have a dominion of their own to exercise it in. The golden rule found no application outside their own contracted sphere. The great God of nations never intended this vast continent of ours for a faction, nor for a sect; it was to be the asylum for the oppressed of every land. The problem of liberty was to be solved in this new world, and all the old world was destined to contribute to its solution. Every new act of oppression on the isles and continent of Europe drove additional exiles to our shores, and every new colony represented a different shade of religious opinion.

 The earliest champion of religious freedom, or "soul liberty," as he designated that most precious jewel of all liberties, was Roger Williams. He came to America on the 5th of February, 1631, to escape the Laudian persecution. He was on terms of intimacy with Oliver Cromwell, and a friend of Milton and Henry Vane, the younger. To him rightly belongs the immortal fame of having been the first person in modern times to assert and maintain in its fullest plenitude the absolute right of every man to "a full liberty in religious concernments," and to found a state wherein this doctrine was the keystone of its organic laws. Before the great Locke advocated the principles of toleration, before Milton wrote his Eiconoclastes, before the patriotic hero and martyr Sidney taught the people the true origin of their rights in his "Discourses Concerning Government," Roger Williams, the first pure type of an American freeman, proclaimed the laws of civil and religious liberty, that "the people were the origin of all free power in government," that God has given to men no power of conscience, nor can men grant this power to each other; that the regulation of the conscience is not one of the purposes for which men combine in civil society. For uttering such heresies this great founder of our liberties was banished from the jurisdiction of the Puritans in America, and driven into the wilderness to endure the severity of our northern winter and the bitter pangs of hunger. For means of subsistence he depended on the Indians, whose trustworthy and trusted friend he became and ever remained. He endeavored at a subsequent period to procure a repeal of the sentence of his banishment, but the rigorous spirit of intolerance prevailed, and the founder of Rhode Island continued till his death an outlaw from Massachusetts.[1]

Some time about June, 1636, Williams, with his five companions, left their frail canoe and came on shore and founded the town, which, in grateful remembrance of "God's merciful providence to him in his distress," he gave the name of Providence. "I desired," said he, "it might be for shelter for persons distressed for conscience." The infant community at Providence at once set about to frame laws for government in strict accord with the spirit of the settlement. All were required to subscribe to the following covenant or constitution: "We, whose names are hereunder written, being desirous of to inhabit in the town of Providence, do promise to submit ourselves in active and passive obedience to all such orders or agreements as shall be made for public good of the body, in an orderly way, by the major consent of the present inhabitants, masters of families incorporated together into a township, and such others as they shall admit into the same, *only in civil things.*" This simple instrument is the earliest constitution of government whereof we have any record, which not only tolerated *all* religions, but recognized as a right, absolute liberty of conscience. The colony at Providence was rapidly increased by the arrival of persons from other colonies, and from Europe, attracted thither by the liberal provisions of its laws and freedom in matters of conscience which

---

[1] Straus's "Roger Williams, the Pioneer of Religious Liberty," Century Co., 1894. John Foord's "Religious Liberty in the United States," *N.Y. Times*, May, 1876.

were there guaranteed. In 1637-8, Portsmouth and Newport were settled, practically as one colony. The settlers were, like Williams, and his companions, exiles or emigrants from Massachusetts. "In imitation of the form of government which existed for a time among the Jews, the inhabitants chose Mr. Coddington to be their magistrate, with the title of Judge; and a few months afterward they elected three elders to assist him."[1] In 1663 a charter was obtained from Charles II., being the second charter of the colony, which continues to the present day to be the fundamental law of the State. It contains this most important provision embodying the principles upon which the colony was founded. "No person within the said colony at any time hereafter shall be any wise molested, punished, disquieted, or called in question for any differences in opinion, in matters of religion, who do not actually disturb the civil peace of our said colony; but that all and every person and persons may from time to time, and at all times hereafter, freely and fully, have and enjoy his own and their judgements and consciences, in matters of religious concernments." Some writers have claimed for Lord Baltimore, proprietor of Maryland, priority in establishing religious liberty on this continent. Undoubted authority, however, proves that not only in point of time did the first laws of Rhode Island in respect to religious liberty precede those of Maryland, but that they also were more comprehensive in their liberality. The first law of Maryland respecting religious liberty was enacted in 1649, while in Rhode Island in 1647 the first

---

[1] "Memoir of Roger Williams," by Prof. Knowles, p. 145.

General Assembly adopted a code of laws, relating exclusively to civil concerns, and concluding with these words: "All men may walk as their consciences persuade them, every one in the name of his God."[1]

Without detracting from the glory of Lord Baltimore, for the liberty he established in Maryland was fully a century in advance of his times, it evidently did not rise to the standard of Rhode Island, in that it extended *only* to Christians.

Having briefly traced the dawn of religious liberty in the smallest of the original colonies, we will now take a view of the religious struggle and its intolerant attitude in the two principal colonies, Virginia and Massachusetts. The colony of Virginia was the first permanent settlement of Englishmen in North America, dating from the founding of Jamestown in 1607. The charter of this colony enjoined the establishment of religion according to the doctrine and usages of the Church of England. Devotion to the Church was a test of loyalty to the King, its "head and defender." In each parish all the inhabitants were taxed alike for the support of the churches of the established order. During the civil war in England, the colony of Virginia, which now had a Legislature of its own, espoused the cause of the King against Cromwell and the Parliament, and hence adhesion to the Estab-

---

[1] For a full discussion of the question see Knowles' "Roger Williams," p. 371. In the light of the most recent investigations the subject has been exhaustively discussed by Sidney S. Rider in his "Rhode Island Historical Tracts," 2d Series, No. 5 (1896). Bancroft in the earlier editions of his history of the United States gave priority to Maryland, but this statement was changed in 1882 and in his last revised edition.

lished Church was made a test of loyalty to the colonial government, and non-conformity was identified with republicanism and disloyalty. The party in power had recourse to religious persecutions, which, as often happens, had more to do with political policy than the question of faith. In the establishment of the "Society for Propagating the Gospel in Foreign Parts," incorporated by act of Parliament, these worldly considerations were not without influence. The conversion of the Indians was its nominal object, but its real purpose was to strengthen the Church of England in America, and to render the colonies duly subservient to England.[1]

---

[1] Hildreth's "History of the U.S.," vol. II., 215, 230, 232. "The most politic of all the schemes that were at this time (1749) proposed in the British cabinet," says Grahame in his "Colonial History of the U.S." (vol. II., 194), "was a project of introducing an ecclesiastical establishment, derived from the model of the Church of England, and particularly the order of bishops, into North America. The pretext assigned for this innovation was, that many non-juring clergymen of the Episcopal persuasion, attached to the cause of the Pretender, had recently emigrated from Britain to America, and that it was desirable to create a board of ecclesiastical dignitaries for the purpose of controlling their proceedings and counteracting their influence; but doubtless it was intended, in part at least, to answer the ends of strengthening royal prerogative in America — of giving to the State, through the Church of England, an accession of influence over the colonists, — and of imparting to their institutions a greater degree of aristocratical character and tendency. The views of the statesmen by whom this design was entertained were inspired by the suggestions of Butler, Bishop of Durham, and were confirmed and seconded by Secker, Archbishop of Canterbury, and the society instituted for the propagation of the gospel. This society had received very erroneous impressions of the religious character of the colonists in general, from some worthless and incapable missionaries, which it sent to America; and Secker, who partook of these impressions, had promulgated them from the pulpit in a strain of vehement and presumptuous invective. Such demeanor by no means tended to conciliate the favor of

Several acts of the Virginia Assembly, of 1659, 1662, and 1693 had made it penal in parents to refuse to have their children baptized. "If no execution took place here," says Mr. Jefferson, "as did in New England, it was not owing to the moderation of the Church, or the spirit of the Legislature, as may be inferred from the law itself; but to historical circumstances which have not been handed down to us."[1] For a century or more the Anglicans retained absolute control, and so long as such was the case the colony was bound hand and foot in political subjection; the ideas of liberty came creeping in with the Dissenters. It has often been observed that when men have restricted and arbitrary laws of church government, they naturally incline to political systems in which all powers of self-government are centralized, and from which the popular element is excluded. The one is a schooling and a precedent for the other. In testimony of this we have a high authority in the Virginia Anglican divine and historian, Boucher: "The constitution of the

---

the Americans to the proposed ecclesiastical establishment. From the intolerance and bitterness of spirit disclosed by the chief promoters of the scheme, it was natural to forebode a total absence of moderation in the conduct of it."

President John Adams, in a letter to Dr. Morse in 1815, referring to this subject, says: "Where is the man to be found at this day, when we see Methodistical bishops, bishops of the Church of England, and bishops and archbishops and Jesuits of the Church of Rome, with indifference, who will believe that the apprehension of Episcopacy contributed, fifty years ago, as much as any other cause, to arouse the attention, not only of the inquiring mind, but of the common people, to close thinking on the constitutional authority of Parliament over the colonies? This, nevertheless, was a fact as certain as any in the history of North America."

[1] Notes on Virginia, Works, vol. VIII., p. 398.

Church of England is approved, confirmed, and adopted by our laws, and interwoven with them. No other form of church government than that of the Church of England would be compatible with the form of our civil government. No other colony has retained so large a portion of the monarchical part of the British constitution as Virginia; and between that attachment to monarchy and the government of the Church of England, there is a strong connection." And again: "A levelling republican spirit in the Church naturally leads to republicanism in the State; neither of which would heretofore have been endured in this ancient dominion."[1] This same author also bears testimony to the approach of Virginia and New England to the same result: "And when it is recollected that till now the opposition to an American episcopate has been confined chiefly to the demagogues and independents of the New England provinces, but that it is now espoused with much warmth by the people of Virginia, it requires no great depth of political sagacity to see what the motives and views of the former have been, or what will be the consequences of the defection of the latter."

The rumor, that the colonies were to be erected into an episcopate of the Established Church, more than once alarmed the people of New England, and, according to John Adams: "The objection was not merely to the office of a bishop, though even that was dreaded, but to the authority of Parliament, on which it must be founded. If

---

[1] Boucher's view, pp. 103-104, from a sermon "On the American Episcopate," preached 1771, in Caroline County, Va.

Parliament can erect dioceses and appoint bishops, they may introduce the whole hierarchy, establish tithes, forbid marriages and funerals, establish religions, forbid dissenters."

In the winter of 1768, the Assembly of Massachusetts appointed a committee to take into consideration the condition of public affairs. The number and names of this committee will show how much importance was attached to their action. It consisted of Mr. Cushing (the Speaker), Colonel James Otis, Mr. Adams, Major Hawley, Mr. Hancock, and four others. This Committee, in its letter to Mr. Deberdt, the agent of the provinces in London, after referring to the establishment of the Catholic religion in Canada, and enumerating the impending evils, come to this grievance: "The establishment of a Protestant episcopate in America is also very zealously contended for; and it is very alarming to a people whose fathers, from the hardships which they suffered under such an establishment, were obliged to fly their native country into a wilderness, in order peaceably to enjoy their privileges, civil and religious. Their being threatened with loss of both at once, must throw them into a disagreeable situation. We hope in God such an establishment will never take place in America, and we desire you would strenuously oppose it. The revenue raised in America, for aught we can tell, may be as constitutionally applied towards the support of prelacy, as of soldiers and pensioners."[1] How the people of Boston were alarmed by such a threatened contingency, is shown by a caricature

---

[1] Tudor's "Life of Otis." p. 307.

in the *Political Register* of 1769, entitled: "An Attempt to Land a Bishop in America." A ship is at the wharf, the lord bishop is in full canonicals, his carriage, crosier, and mitre on deck, the people appear with a banner inscribed with "Liberty and Freedom of Conscience," and are shouting, "No lords, spiritual or temporal, in New England." "Shall they be obliged to maintain bishops that cannot maintain themselves?" They pelt the bishop with Locke, Sidney on Government, Barclay's Apology, Calvin's Works, and the unhappy prelate has mounted the shrouds, ejaculating, "Lord, now Lord, lettest thou thy servant depart in peace."[1] The Society for the Propagation of the Gospel in Foreign Parts was active in this scheme for establishing the Church through an American episcopate. In October, 1776, Dr. Charles Inglis, Rector of Trinity Church, New York, wrote to the society: "The present rebellion is certainly one of the most causeless, unprovoked, and unnatural that ever disgraced any country. Although civil liberty was the ostensible object, yet it is now past all doubt that an abolition of the Church of England was one of the principal springs of the dissenting leaders' conduct." He further asserts that "All the society's missionaries in New Jersey, New York, Connecticut, have proven themselves faithful, loyal subjects," shutting up their churches rather than cease praying for the King, and he urges the establishment of the episcopate as an encouragement to such fidelity.[2] William Tudor, in his "Life of James Otis," wherein he dwells

---

[1] See the picture in Thornton's Pulpit of the American Revolution.
[2] "Doc. Hist. of New York," III., 637.

quite fully on the contemporary events from 1760 to 1775, says: "A jealousy of the designs of the English hierarchy was kept constantly alive by the indications given from time to time of anxiety to extend its authority over this country, and by the indiscreet conduct of some of its missionaries. Fear, hatred, and a long course of hereditary prejudice against this church, combined almost all the dissenting clergy of New England against it, and naturally led them to sympathize with those who opposed the constitutional acts of political power."

To return to Virginia. In 1755 a short crop of tobacco having suddenly enhanced the price, the Assembly passed a temporary act authorizing the payment of debts, instead of in tobacco, as heretofore, in money at twopence for the pound of tobacco. Three years after, this tender act was renewed. The salaries of the parish ministers, some sixty-five in number, were payable in tobacco. As they were considerable losers by this act, they sent an agent to England, and by the aid of Sherlock, Bishop of London, procured an order in council pronouncing the law void. Suits were immediately brought to recover the difference between twopence per pound and the value of the tobacco. Patrick Henry was one of those engaged to plead against "the parsons." The contract was that Maury, "the parson," should be paid sixteen thousand pounds of tobacco. The act of 1758 fixed the value at twopence per pound; it was worth thrice that sum in 1759. The question of law at issue was simply this: the act of 1758 having been duly and regularly enacted, could it be annulled by the King in Council? As interpreted by Henry, it was a question between the prerogative and the people of Virginia. He defined the uses of the Established Church and to what extent obedience is due the King. "Except you are disposed," are his words, "yourselves to rivet the chains of bondage on your own necks, do not let slip the opportunity now offered of making such an example of the reverend plaintiff, as shall hereafter be a warning to himself and his brothers not to have the temerity to dispute the validity of laws authenticated by the only sanction which can give force to laws for the government of this colony, the authority of its own legal representatives, with its council and governor." The jury promptly rendered a verdict of a penny damages, and it had the effect, as prophesied by the Bishop of London, who said: "The rights of the clergy and the authority of the King must stand or fall together." Thus, singularly enough, it united ecclesiastical and constitutional questions as causes of the revolution in Virginia, as they had been united in Massachusetts from the beginning of her settlement.[1] And the same sparks of liberty that were kindled by Otis in Boston in 1761, in his argument against writs of assistance, were ignited anew in Virginia by Patrick Henry in the "parson's case."

When the revolution came, we find the Baptists and Presbyterians were almost to a man in its favor, influenced by dual considerations, civil and ecclesiastical, by

---

[1] See Hon. Mellen Chamberlain's address on John Adams, before the Webster Historical Society, January 18, 1884. (Published by the Society, Boston) Brooks Adams's "Emancipation of Massachusetts" (1887), pp. 319, 341.

the hope of seeing in the success of the revolution the overthrow of an establishment which they regarded with fear and repugnance. Under such conditions, it was naturally to be expected that assaults on the Established Church would be made, and they were made, not without success. At its first meeting after the Declaration, the Presybtery of Hanover, in Virginia, addressed the Virginia House of Assembly a memorial recommending, in a spirit of fairness and equal justice to all, a separation of Church and State, leaving the support of the gospel to the voluntary efforts of its votaries. "In this enlightened age," runs the memorial, "and in a land where all of every denomination are united in the most strenuous efforts to be free, we hope and expect that our representatives will cheerfully concur in removing every species of religious as well as civil bondage. Certain it is, that every argument for civil liberty gains additional strength when applied to liberty in the concerns of religion." From this memorial it would appear, that in the opinion of these memorialists, a majority of the population of Virginia were Episcopalians. Mr. Jefferson, on the other hand, states that two thirds of the people had become dissenters at the commencement of the revolution. "I am inclined to think," says Robert Baird,[1] "that the greater part professed or favored Episcopacy, but that a decided majority were opposed to its civil establishment." Mr. Jefferson was the great champion of religious liberty, and he advocated the cause with a devotion and fervor of purpose that carried before it every opposition; but it was

---

[1] Baird's "Religion in America," p. 220.

not until the winter of 1785-6, ten years after the beginning of the revolution, that an act for establishing religious freedom was adopted in Virginia, and the last vestige of a united Church and State was obliterated.[1]

The plan of an Established Church, according to Rev. Robert Baird, was at one time adopted in all the American States except Pennsylvania and Rhode Island. The nature of the establishment, however, varied in the different States. In Massachusetts, Connecticut, New York, Virginia, and South Carolina it was almost as strict as in England. The early efforts to promote religious liberty in Virginia doubtless had its direct influence in the other colonies. In November, 1776, measures to the same effect were adopted by the legislature of Maryland, and the union of Church and State was in a like manner dissolved by the Legislatures in New York, South Carolina, and all the other colonies in which the Protestant Episcopal church was predominant. Of all these States, Connecticut and Massachusetts were the last to yield to the advancing spirit of religious liberty. It was not till 1816 that the connection was dissolved in the former, and not till 1833 that the finishing blow was given to it in the latter State. The religious complexion of no two of the American colonies was precisely alike. The various sects at the time of the revolution were grouped as follows: The Puritans in Massachusetts, the Baptists in Rhode Island, the Congregationalists in Connecticut, the Duch and Swedish Protestants in New Jersey, the Church of England in

---

[1] See Act for Establishing Religious Freedom, Jefferson's Works, vol. VIII., 454.

New York, the Quakers in Pennsylvania, the Baptists, Methodists, and Presbyterians in North Carolina, the Catholics in Maryland, the Cavaliers in Virginia, the Huguenots and Episcopalians in South Carolina, and the Methodists in Georgia. Owing to these fortunate diversities, to the consciousness of dangers from ecclesiastical ambition, the intolerance of sects as exemplified among themselves as well as in foreign lands, it was wisely foreseen that the only basis upon which it was possible to form a Federal union was to exclude from the National Government all power over religion. "It was impossible that there should not arise perpetual strife and perpetual jealousy," says Judge Story, "if the National Government were left free to create a religious establishment. But this alone would have been an imperfect security, if it had not been followed up by a declaration of the right of the free exercise of religion, and a prohibition of all religious tests."[1]

It is fair to presume that no one sect a hundred years ago, if it had possessed the exclusive power, would have

---

[1] Story on the Constitution, § 1879. Mr. Jefferson, when President, wrote the following letter, in 1802, to the Danbury Baptist Association: "Believing with you, that religion is a matter which lies solely between man and his God, that he owes account to none for his faith or his worship, that the legislative powers of government reach action only, and not opinions, I contemplate with sovereign reverence that act of the whole American people which declared that their Legislature should 'make no law respecting an establishment of religion or prohibiting the free exercise thereof,' thus building a wall of separation between Church and State. Adhering to this expression of the supreme will of the nation in behalf of the rights of conscience, I shall see with sincere satisfaction the progress of those sentiments which tend to restore to man all his natural rights, convinced that he has no natural right in opposition to his social duties."

established by law, absolute religious liberty for all sects. When, therefore, we trace the origin of religious liberty as guaranteed by the Constitution, it is erroneous to ascribe it to the acts or liberal tendencies of any one or more particular sects. On the contrary, the credit belongs as much to the intolerant as to the tolerant sects. The constitutional provisions on this subject clearly bear the marks not of mutual concessions, but of reciprocal distrust. That there was good ground for such distrust, the provisions of the early constitutions of several of the States on the subject of religion bear ample testimony. And even to this day the Constitution or laws of several of the States require a belief in the being of a God, and in a future state of rewards and punishments as a qualification for holding civil office and for testifying in a court of justice. But these laws are fast falling into disuse. The laws of the States of North Carolina and Maryland have within recent years been modified in this respect. At rare intervals even at the present day we see cropping up the old spirit of intolerance in efforts to desecularize the public schools, or in a bill offered in the Legislature to convert a sectarian holiday into a secular *dies non*. These attempts are generally predicated upon the false basis that Christianity is in some way a part of our laws, or on the Protestant majority claim. As to the first claim, Jefferson clearly disproved that, by a careful examination of the ancient authorities upon which the claim was supposed to rest. "We may safely affirm," says he, "that Christianity neither is, nor ever was, a part of the common law.[1] The treaty adopted between the United States and Tripoli on Nov. 4, 1796, and signed by Washington, recites in the eleventh article, as a reason why harmony with that Mohammedan country could be preserved, that "the government of the United States is not in any sense founded on the Christian religion."[2]

A word only as to the second claim, that of the Protestant majority, which says the majority religion in this country being the Protestant, and the majority of Protestants being in favor of reading the Protestant Bible in the public schools and the like, therefore the minority ought to submit. The answer to this argument is, that while in political matters the majority rules, in matters of religion and of conscience, our Federal and State constitutions delegate no such authority, and the majority possesses no such power as to discriminate against a minority however small. To such as would ask why religion was left out of the Constitution? we answer in the words of Washington, "Because it belonged to the churches, and not to the State."[3]

---

[1] Letter to Thomas Cooper (1814), Works, vol. VI., 311.

[2] For other authorities see Vidal *vs.* Girard Executors, 2 How., 198; Andrew *vs.* Bible Society, 4 Sandford, 182; Cooley on Constitutional Limitations, p. 472; Bloom *vs.* Richards' Ohio State Rep., 387, also Minor *vs.* Board of Education in Cincinnati (1870). See Arguments in same case by J.B. Stallo, George Hoadley, and Stanley Matthews, counsel for defendants (published by Rob't Clark & Co., Cincinnati, O.).

[3] Letter in *Massachusetts Sentinel*, Dec. 5, 1789, to the Presbyterians of New Hampshire and Massachusetts, who complained of "the omission of God" in the Constitution.

CHAPTER IV.

The Genesis of the Republic

The social, religious, and political upheavals that kept the governments of England and the Continent in constant change and commotion, had as yet little effect in the colonies. The people here were busy with their own affairs, and England having not as yet laid her rapacious hands upon them, they prospered all the more by reason of this neglect. Beliefs that had lost much of their vigor in Europe retained all their ancient force in the colonies. The inestimable privilege of worshipping God in accordance with their own conscience was denied to the first settlers of New England in the mother country, and they came to the wilds of America to enjoy that boon. The Bible was to them not only their guide in religion, but their textbook in politics. They studied the Old Testament and applied its teaching with a thoroughness and literal devotion that no people, excepting only the Jews, and perhaps the Scotch, had ever exemplified, for they seemed to recognize a striking similarity between their own hardships, history, and condition and those of the children of Israel under Moses and Joshua. They quoted its texts with a literal application. Their condition they characterized as "Egyptian Bondage," James I. they styled "Pharaoh," the ocean whose dangers and hardships their ancestors were driven to encounter they spoke of as the "Red Sea." They likened their own numbers to that of the children of Israel, "three million souls," America in whose wilds they had come was their "Wilderness," and in after days Washington and Adams were frequently referred to as their Moses and Joshua. Their first conception of the form of an American union was a Theocracy, the same form of government in all its essential characteristics, and expressly modelled thereafter, as the children of Israel set up over the twelve tribes under their great lawgiver Moses. They continued this Theocracy for a period of forty-one years, from 1643 to 1684, and under it they organized the New England Confederacy. "This confederacy of the four New England Colonies," says Pitkin, "served as the basis of the great confederacy afterwards between the thirteen States of America."[1] An examination of the two systems discloses a similarity not only in name, but in principles. The Puritans, especially the New England Puritans, evinced a greater preference for the Old Testament than perhaps they themselves were aware of. The persecutions they had suffered in the mother country instead of subduing or disbanding them, had transformed them from what at first was a sect into a faction, united together by the strongest ties of union with spirits rendered more determined by the severity of

---

[1] Pitkin's "History of the U. S." vol. I., p. 52.

the hardships they had endured. The wilderness they had conquered by their patient toil was now blossoming as a garden interspersed within growing villages and populous towns. Their first and only concern was to preserve this new Canaan for themselves, and to establish such laws and regulations for their government as might secure this end beyond peradventure. The Mosaic laws were framed under divine sanction to accomplish a similar end. To these laws they turned as a guide, not taking into account that more than thirty centuries had rolled by, and that the social regulations of those times were no better fitted for the then times than the vestments of that clime would suffice as a proper protection against the New England winter. They did not seem to understand that however severe the Mosaic code was, it was mild in comparison with the laws that preceded it, and that the social relations of mankind had undergone a change during the many centuries that had rolled by. They even baptized their children no longer by the names of Christian saints but by those of the Hebrew prophets and patriarchs. In a word, they adopted not the spirit but the letter of the Old Testament, and here was the radical error of their social regulations.[1]

The question suggests itself: Why could not the social laws and religious regulations of the Hebrews be adopted by the people of New England with the same propriety, justice, and applicability as their form of government? The answer is plain. The former were framed upon the central idea of exclusiveness. The children of Israel were,

---

[1] See notes, page 111.

as they believed, God's chosen people. Social and religious regulations were made with this chief end in view, that they might not by contact with surrounding nations lapse into idolatry. On the other hand, their form of government was constructed upon laws of universal humanity, upon the broad principles that all men are equal, that God alone is King; which were as true when the Declaration of Independence was adopted as in the times of Moses and Joshua, and as true in New England as they were in Canaan.

Early in the history of the American people, Cotton Mather, who was an extreme Old Testamentarian, said: "New England being a country whose interests are remarkably enwrapped in ecclesiastical circumstances, ministers ought to concern themselves in politics." Verily they followed his advice. They mustered not only in the ranks of the Continental army, with their firelocks in hand, fighting the battles of the revolution, but on Sunday their eloquent voices were heard from the pulpit and in camp denouncing not only as false in principle, but as against the true spirit and meaning of the Scriptures, the slavish doctrines of "unlimited submission and non-resistance," which, they explained, had been invented by crown sycophants and court chaplains to flatter the ears of tyrannical rulers. They pictured in glowing words the rise and fall of the Hebrew Commonwealth, and read to their hearers again and again the warnings and admonitions of Samuel, and the references made by the prophets to the wrongs and injustice of kings, and the consequential sufferings of the people because of their rejecting

God's established rule, the government of the people as it existed under Moses, Joshua, and the Judges. "And the Lord said unto Samuel, hearken unto the voice of the people in all that they say unto thee; for they have not rejected thee, but they have rejected me, that I should not rule over them" (Samuel viii., 7). "Now therefore hearken unto their voice: howbeit yet protest solemnly unto them, and show them the manner of the king that shall reign over them" (*Id.*, 9.) These and similar passages were taken as texts for the politico-theological sermons that were heard Sunday after Sunday throughout New England. Jonathan Mayhew, in the preface to his famous discourse "Concerning Unlimited Submission and Non-Resistance to Higher Powers," etc., published at the request of the hearers, delivered on the 30th of January, 1750, the anniversary of the death of King Charles I., says by way of introduction: "It is to be hoped that but few will think the subject an improper one to be discoursed on in the pulpit, under a notion that this is preaching politics, instead of Christ. Why then should not these parts of the Scripture which relate to civil government be examined and explained from the desk as well as others?"

By a remarkable and potent coincidence the very texts and arguments drawn from the Scriptures, that were adduced by the divines to resist the unjust exactions and illegal encroachments of the king, and which stripped the royal sceptre of its divine character, held up before the American people the Hebrew Commonwealth as a model of government; — so closely are the rights of the people and their form of government identified in the books of the Old Testament. The same Scriptural records which weaned the Americans from their monarchical affiliations, which placed the divine mark upon popular government, and which designated *that form* as best calculated to secure the inestimable privileges of civil liberty, also supplied the model for its creation.

We must not forget that in our colonial period the great majority of people had neither the leisure nor the facilities for acquiring knowledge which they have in our day. The ability to read was a much rarer accomplishment than now; newspapers were few, and those few were weekly publications, while books were relatively expensive. The pulpit occupied a more general sphere, and exerted much greater influence. Ministers preached politics as well as religion. The pulpit was the most direct way of reaching the people.

As early as 1633 the governor and assistants in the New England colonies began to appoint the most eloquent and distinguished ministers to preach on the day of the general election. The sermon was styled the election sermon. On these occasions political subjects were not only permissible, but specially appropriate. The sermon was printed, every representative receiving several copies, and it was distributed throughout the colonies. By the charter of William and Mary, in 1691, the last Wednesday in May was set apart as "Election Day," and it remained so until the revolution. The sermons preached on this day are remarkable for their learning and political wisdom. One cannot fail on reading them to recognize the fact that they contributed much of the moral force that brought about our independence. "The publication of these sermons in pamphlet form was a part of the regular proceedings of the Assembly. Scattered over the land, clothed with the double sanction of their distinguished authorship and the endorsement of the Legislature, they became the textbooks of human rights, and in every parish they were regarded as the political pamphlets of the day."[1] In 1774, when our whole country was in misery, in the travail which preceded the birth of the nation, the first provincial Congress of Massachusetts acknowledged with profound gratitude the public obligations to the ministers as friends of civil and religious liberty, and invoked their aid to assist "in avoiding the dreadful slavery with which we are not threatened, and for the establishment of the rights and liberties of America."

The framers of the Republic of the United States did not construct this government after the model of any of the then existing republics, or after that of the great republics of classical or medieval history. They brought to their aid the experiences of all the past; the entire science of government was their guide. In the words of Franklin, who, as an authority on this subject, is second to none: "We have gone back to ancient history for models of government, and examined the different forms of those republics which, having been originally formed with the

---

[1] "Chaplains and Clergy of the Revolution," J.T. Headley. See J. Wingate Thornton's excellent compilation, "The Pulpit of the American Revolution," Boston, 1876.

seeds of their own dissolution, now no longer exist; and we have viewed modern states all round Europe, but find none of their constitutions suitable to our own circumstances."[1] On the other hand, the departments constituting the framework of our government — the executive, legislative, and judicial, — owe their origin directly to similar departments in the government of England, and to the general form of construction of the then existing colonial governments. In the spirit and essence of our Constitution the influence of the Hebrew Commonwealth was paramount, in that it was not only the highest authority for the principle: "Rebellion to Tyrants is obedience to God," but also because it was in itself a divine precedent for a pure democracy as distinguished from monarchy, aristocracy, or any other form of government. By that means and to that extent it had a decisive influence in guiding the American people in the selection of their form of government.

After the termination of the war between France and England for dominion in America, when the question of separation from England was first forced upon the minds of the colonists, republics were not looked upon with favor. It was not a democratic age. The inscription upon the little desk upon which the Declaration of Independence was penned, tells the whole story in these characteristic words: "Politics as well as religion has its superstitions." And those superstitions were not on the side of popular government. Superstition always lurks about the dark and mysterious, it is founded in igno-

---

[1] Bigelow's "Franklin," vol. III., p. 388.

rance, fostered by habit and promoted by regal authority. The main bulwarks of the kingly power were these very superstitions which surrounded the kingly person and prerogatives, and no means were more effective in freeing the minds of the masses from them than the history of the liberation of the children of Israel and the development of their democratic government. Prudent and conservative men are naturally more inclined to adopt institutions with which they are familiar and under which they have lived, than to work experiments in untried projects or utopian theories. The colonists were accustomed to a monarchical form of government. This form was much preferred by the people at large to that of a democracy. All the so-called democracies of history had been subverted or perverted, so that the privileged few had arrogated to themselves even greater powers than a king ever dared practically to assume. Such had been the result under the Grecian, Roman, and Venetian republics, and in the republics of Holland and England in a modified form. In all of these so-called republics, the government theoretically was founded on the supremacy of the people, but the power was exercised in a manner to defeat its purpose. They were, in the language of Gibbon, in his description of the Roman Commonwealth, "Absolute monarchies disguised in the form of a Commonwealth." It was argued with great historical force, that the people of England had been in a state of turmoil and unrest during the entire period of the Commonwealth, and that their liberties were more secure under the Restoration than they had been under the Commonwealth.

Montesquieu derided "this impotent effort of the English to establish a democracy," and pointed out the true causes of its failure. "The government was incessantly changed, and the astonished people sought for democracy, and found it nowhere. After much violence and many shocks and blows they were fain to fall back on the same government they had overthrown."

The English Commonwealth was most familiar to the people of the colonies, its rise and subversion were chapters in their own history, and every American, as well as every Englishman, recognized the fact that this commonwealth as an experiment in popular government, was a complete failure, for otherwise the Restoration would never have taken place. Aside from that, the people in England during the Commonwealth feared the sovereignty of Parliament more than they ever did that of the King. "The Commons were a sort of collective, self-constituted, perpetual dictatorship like Rome under the Decemviri. England was enslaved by its legislators; they were irresponsible, absolute, and apparently not to be dissolved but at their own pleasure."[1] While it is true that the colonies during the period of the Commonwealth were comparatively happy in the enjoyment of the privilege of being let alone, yet the circumstances that brought about its overthrow had the natural effect of discouraging a like attempt, or any attempt to establish a republic. Its failure was cited and referred to as a practi-

---

[1] Bancroft's "History of the U.S.," vol. I., p. 391.

cal argument and illustration in favor of the kingly rule. The troubled condition of the then existing republics was not such as to invite imitation of their form of government. The Republic of Holland was in a very precarious state, so much so that Mr. Adams says of it in his "Defence of the Constitutions of Government": "Considering the critical situation of it, prudence dictates to pass it over."[1] Thee same observations apply even with greater force to the Republic of Venice, which at that time showed signs of dissolution, and soon thereafter, in 1797, after having endured longer than the republics of Rome or Sparta, or any other history, ceased to exist. In the following year, 1799, Genoa met with a similar fate, its government having been finally overthrown by the allied armies of France. The Swiss Confederation, although it had existed for centuries, did not invite imitation, in that it was aristocratic in its tendencies, and more especially because the different cantons were continually at variance one with another to such an extent that political authors have justly ascribed its long preservation not to any inherent cohesion or stability of its own, but to the menacing attitude of surrounding nations, which presented to the various cantons a common danger, and

---

[1] Works of John Adams, vol. IV., p. 356. "The government of Holland grew out of the immediate necessities of the heroic struggle with the power of Spain. It never could be presented as a model for imitation by any people; it was a singular combination of corporation and aristocratical influence with a federal principle. The author had good reason for avoiding at the moment of publication any analysis of a system which was then crumbling, and which has since been swept completely away." — p. 357. Note, by Charles Francis Adams.

thereby had the effect to continue and cement a Confederation which otherwise would have broken asunder. Even the Republic of Carthage which resembled the Hebrew Commonwealth more than any other of the republics of history, and which, according to John Adams, also resembled those of the States of America more closely than any of the ancient, and perhaps more than any of the modern republics, was not a pure democracy, in that birth and wealth were necessary qualifications for the offices of Senator, Pentarch, and Suffete. These two qualifications, however, were not all-sufficient; merit was indispensable, and for that reason it rises above most of the other ancient republics, so that even Aristotle bestowed the highest praise upon its form of government. "It is a general opinion that the Carthaginians live under a polity which is excellent and in many respects superior to all others."[1]

The Hebrew Commonwealth, unlike the other republics, both ancient and modern, was an original government. It was not constructed from the remnants of a shattered monarchy, nor did it belong to that class of governments which were "originally formed from the seeds of their own dissolution." The governing power was exercised by the people, and not arrogated by the few, or retained by aristocratic families who might thereby have the means of constituting themselves an heredity senate. The children of Israel, when they escaped from the thraldom of Pharaoh, like the people of America when they severed their allegiance from the

---

[1] Politics of Aristotle, book II., ch. 2.

king, were peculiarly fortunate in having no titled classes with exclusive privileges to contend against, no institutions among them which had outlived their usefulness, no old ruins to rebuild. They were peculiarly fortunate in having the power of organizing for themselves such form of government as they in their most deliberate judgement, guided by the experiences of all nations, might elect. It may be an accidental coincidence that in the history of these two people there should exist so many circumstances that bear a striking similarity to one another, that in respect to government they should have arrived at the same result, the establishment of a federal democratic republic. Yet it is doubtless more in accord with the logic of history, which is "philosophy teaching by example," to conclude that the former was a material element in the genesis of the latter, and a positive influence in its national formation aside from any direct connection we may succeed in tracing in these pages.

CHAPTER V.

Monarchy and the Church

The primitive Christians derived the institution of civil government, not from the consent of the people, but from the decrees of God. The king or emperor was the Deity's vicegerent. The public establishment of Christianity by Constantine in the beginning of the fourth century had the effect of placing the altar on the throne, and the ultimate result was the desecration of the one and the degradation of the other. It carried with it as a state doctrine the unconditional submission on the part of the governed to the powers that be, as preached by the apostle in the reign of Nero. While the establishment in its inception may have had the effect of fostering and spreading the light of the new faith in the pagan world, it proved on the other hand a hindrance to the development of civil liberty for twelve centuries and more, distinct traces of which are yet to be found in the despotic governments of the Old World. Its immediate consequences were the augmentation of the power of the Pope and the subjection of every Christian country, in matters temporal as well as ecclesiastical, to the throne of Peter. What countless miseries might have been spared mankind had Constantine been permitted to live and die a pagan, and what effect the continued separation of Church and State would have had on the destinies of the nations of the earth, are subjects suggesting a drift of historical speculation that would doubtless be replete with most interesting deductions. This, however, we must leave to the consideration of others.[1]

Aside from the countless benefits that flow from Protestantism in all countries, we must not lose sight of the fact that Protestantism in England had its origin under Henry VIII., so far as the King himself was concerned, in motives that are not to be commended. He embraced the cause not from any noble purposes, not to secure thereby greater liberty for his loyal subjects, but to procure greater license for himself. The power of the Pope, against which he rebelled, he arrogated to himself, and thereby united in his prerogatives Church and State. "Popedom was, after the rupture had been consummated through the folly of Pope Pius the V., virtually effaced from the national Christianity. So serious a void there

---

[1] "Whoever governs you his religion shall be yours! *Cujus regio, ejus religio.* Were ever more blasphemous and insulting words hurled in the face of mankind? Yet this was accepted as the net result of the Reformation, so far as priests and princes could settle the account. This was the ingenious compromise by which it was thought possible to remove the troublesome question of religious forever from the sphere of politics . . . Not freedom of religion, but freedom of princes to prescribe religion to their slaves — for this so many tens of thousands had died on the battlefield, or been burned and buried alive!" — John Lothrop Motley, in a lecture entitled "Historic Progress," delivered before the N.Y. Historical Society, in 1868.

was a temptation, perhaps a necessity, to fill, and through the force of events more than any formal declaration, it was filled in the main by the sovereign. This was a result extremely adverse to civil freedom. It further heightened the excess of regal power which had already marked the Tudor period. The doctrines of Divine Right and of passive obedience took deep root in England, and they were peculiarly the growth of the English Reformation."[1]

This unfortunate union of Church and State, of the crosier and the sword, has been the prime source of more bloodshed in Europe than all other causes combined. In England, besides contributing to the circumstances that gave rise to the independent party which brought Charles I. to the scaffold., it created the schism between the Crown and the Puritans. This schism drove many of the latter to America, in order that they might there enjoy liberty of conscience, which was denied them under the Established Church; and this in turn, by the alarm occasioned by the frequent attempts to create an established church throughout America, contributed in no slight degree to political liberty and the severing of the connection between colonies and the mother country.[2]

---

[1] Right Honorable W.E. Gladstone, *Contemporary Review*, October, 1878.

[2] "Independence of English Church and State was the fundamental principle of the first colonists, has been its general principle for two hundred years, and now we hope is past dispute. Who then was the author, inventor, discoverer of Independence? The only true answer must be, the first emigrants; and the proof of it is, the charter of James the I. When wee say that Otis, Adams, Mayhew, Henry, Lee, Jefferson, etc., were authors of independence, we ought to say they were only awakeners and revivers of the

When we consider that the prime motives of the first settlers in New England were not for commerce, nor for worldly gain, nor for civil dominion, but to secure for themselves liberty of worship, we can understand why it was, and should be, that these people were constantly on their guard against every act and move of the mother country which in the remotest degree might ultimately lead to an abridgment of this sacred right. Lord Chatham, in his celebrated letter to the king, wrote: "They left their native land in search of freedom, and found it in a desert. Divided as they are into a thousand forms of politics and religion, there is one point in which they all agree, they equally detest the pageantry of a king and the supercilious hypocrisy of a bishop."

The doctrine of "Divine Right" had a deep-rooted significance, and held great sway among those who were communicants of the Established Church. It signified that the king could do no wrong; that whatever sufferings the people might be subjected to by reason of the king's tyranny and cruelty, it was but proper that the people should bear them with meekness, for did not the Apostle say: "Let every soul be subject unto the higher powers, for there is no power but of God. The powers that be are ordained of God," which signified that in no case should the people resist their lawful sovereign, no matter what inroads he might make upon their most sacred rights and unalienable privileges. The duty of a subject is under every and all circumstances "unlimited

---

original fundamental principle of colonization." — Works of John Adams, vol. X., p. 359.

submission" and "non-resistance"; for did not the Apostle say: "Whosoever, therefore, resisteth the power resisteth the ordinance of God, and they that resist shall receive to themselves damnation." It was further maintained that the king's cruelty, tyranny, and oppression was for the good of the people. It was a means God employed to punish them for transgressions: "For he is the minister of God, a revenger to execute wrath upon him that doeth evil; therefore, ye must needs be subject not only for wrath, but also for conscience' sake."[1] "What, then," it was asked, "can there no case happen wherein the people may of right, and by their own authority, help themselves; take up arms and set upon their king imperiously domineering over them? None at all whilst he remains a king. 'Honor the king,' and 'He that resisteth resists the ordinance of God,' are divine oracles that will never permit it."[2]

Such were the theories of government and of civil and religious liberty that were prevalent among the ecclesiastics of the Established Church under James I., and the king was not slow in availing himself of this great badge of absolutism, sanctified by the title of "Divine Right." Sir Robert Filmer, who was to James I. what Bossuet was to Louis XIV., the standard bearer of the rankest kind of absolutism, possessing a great mind cramped by a superstitious age, formulated these theories into a system which, according to Macaulay, became the badge of the

---

[1] The words in quotation are from Romans, chap. xiii., 1-6.
[2] Cited by Locke on Civil Government (Lib. II., 237) from Barclay's Contra Monarchomachos.

vilest class of Tories and High Churchmen. It soon found many advocates among those who aspired to the king's favor, and made rapid progress among the clergy of the Established Church.[1] The execution of Charles I. naturally gave a great check to the doctrine of "Divine Right," as well as to the whole system of ecclesiastical authority, and to every form of absolutism, but the change was too sudden to be durable; a reaction was destined to come, and soon after the Restoration many began to regard the late king as a martyr, and the day of his death was made one of the sacred days, solemnized as a day of fasting and humiliation by way of court and compliment to King Charles II.

Thus the people sought to ingratiate themselves with the Crown at the expense of their liberties, and yielded freely to Charles II. the very liberties they beheaded Charles I. for usurping. The ecclesiastics made a strenuous effort to recover their former power, to revive and reinforce the doctrine of "Divine Right." On the day of the execution of Lord William Russell, in 1683, the University of Oxford declared: "Submission and obedience clear, absolute and without exception, to be the badge and character of the Church of England." An act was passed by Parliament which acknowledged not only that the military power was exclusively in the king, but declared that in no extremity whatever could Parliament be justified in withstanding him by force. Another act had passed which required every officer of a corporation to receive the Eucharist according to the rites of the Church

---

[1] History of England, vol. I., chap. 1.

of England, and to swear that he held resistance to the king's authority to be in all case unlawful. About the same time the bishops were restored to their seats in the House of Lords. The Church of England, in return for the protection it received from the crown, was not ungrateful. She had from her birth been attached to Monarchy, but during the quarter of a century that followed the Restoration, her zeal for royal authority and hereditary right passed all bounds. She accordingly magnified every element of prerogative. Her favorite theme was the doctrine of Non-Resistance. That doctrine she taught without exception or qualification, and followed out to all its extreme consequences.

These considerations would not be of interest in this connection, were it not that the effect of all such movements was strongly felt in the American colonies, and had great weight among a large and influential class of Episcopalians, "in such a manner as to undermine all the principles of liberty, whether civil or religious."[1] And from the further fact that the adherence to or dissent from the doctrine of "passive obedience and non-resistance" in America distinctly divided the Loyalists from the Whigs. Our authority for this statement is the distinguished Anglican divine and historian of the revolution, Jonathan Boucher, who, in a discourse delivered in the latter end of 1775, in the parish of Queen Anne, in Maryland, "On Civil Liberty, Passive Obedience, and

---

[1] Jonathan Mayhew's discourse concerning Unlimited Submission and Non-Resistance to Higher Power, etc., delivered in West Meeting House, Boston, January 30, 1750.

Non-Resistance," after referring to the meaning of that doctrine as applied to the present duty of the colonies as towards the mother country, says: "It really is a striking feature in our national history, that ever since the Revolution, hardly any person of any note has preached or published a sermon into which it was possible to drag this topic without declaring against this doctrine. It seems to have been made a kind of criterion or test of principle and the watchword of a party. What is not less remarkable is, that whilst the right of resistance has thus incessantly been delivered from the pulpit, insisted on by orators, and inculcated by statesmen, the contrary position is still (I believe) the dictate of religion and certainly the doctrine of the Established Church, and still also the law of the land."[1]

The Episcopalians, as a class, in New England and in the other colonies, warmly espoused the cause of the Crown; as they derived their ecclesiastical authority from the Church of England, loyalty to the king was a part of their worship, and this fact was seized upon and was utilized by the Crown, through its colonial governors, from political as well as religious motives. George III., before the time when the crisis arrived in America, had revived in all its force the monstrous doctrine of "Divine Right," which the revolution was supposed to have destroyed. He had the most exalted notions of his own prerogatives,

---

[1] From a discourse by Jonathan Boucher in answer to a sermon on the same text and subject by the Rev. Mr. Duché, preached and printed in Philadelphia in July, 1775. — "American Revolution," by Boucher, pp. 495 and 545.

and to his despotic temper was added an overweening sense of the homage due him as head of the Church. This phase of George's character little concerned the people of Great Britain, as British liberty was secure, carefully guarded by constitutional limitations and by their representatives in the House of Commons. The position of America was entirely different in this respect. The royal theory as to colonies was, that they were Crown dependencies. The people had no representative in Parliament or at the court to look after their interests, and no one to guard them from injustice, excepting a Pitt or a Barré, and a few others like them, whose sense of right and equality impelled them to disregard party affiliations, and to plead the cause of the outraged colonists.

In Great Britain any attempted encroachment of the king or his ministers upon the rights of the people could be checked by the Commons, but as toward the colonists the king and Parliament were on the same side, and absolutism had full reign, limited only by the power of resistance in self-defense, which the people in the colonies, goaded by the wrongs and injustice they had suffered, might be able to command. The result was, as has already been stated; under different conditions the Revolution of 1688 was reenacted in America. The arguments of Filmer and Hobbes were again opposed by those of Sidney and Locke. The doctrine of "Divine Right and Unlimited Submission," as distorted from the New Testament, was battered down by the laws of Moses and the admonitions of Samuel as contained in the Old. Puritan theology was arrayed against the politico-theological tenets of the Established Church. The divine supremacy of the Law, as embodied in and illustrated by the Hebrew Commonwealth, was brought in conflict with the "Divine Right" of kings, as exhibited in the absolutism of George III., and out of this struggle came to life American Liberty.

CHAPTER VI.

The Hebrew Commonwealth, The First Federal Republic [1]

The historians and writers on political science, in tracing the origin of democratic government, refer invariably to the republics of Greece, assuming that civil liberty was first cradled there under their Solons and Lycurguses. We must look farther back than either Athens or Sparta for the origin of the blessings which we enjoy, and which are guaranteed to us under the forms of popular government. The form of government outlined by Moses and practically developed under Joshua and his successors, first embodied the principles upon which the rights and liberties of a people should rest and be sustained. The Hebrew Commonwealth originated and organized a civil polity which the matured experience of after-ages selected as the most perfect from of government. The best features of the Greek and Roman republics, and as I

---

[1] See notes, page 111.

shall attempt to show of our American republic, were exhibited, not in dim outline, but in many respects in quite an advanced stage of development, in this the first of democratic republics.

The Hebrew Commonwealth embraces that period of the history of the children of Israel, from the Exodus to the selection of Saul as king; that is, during the administration of Moses, Joshua, and the Judges, about 550 years, according to the generally approved chronology from about 1650 B.C. to 1099 B.C. That the Israelites while in Egypt were under some definite discipline and regulations of their own, is to be inferred not only from the fact that when they left Egypt they did not go forth like a tumultuous rabble, but marched as an organized army under regular leaders, but also from the circumstance that when Moses was first sent to deliver God's message to the children of Israel, he was directed to "gather the elders of Israel together," and he literally followed this express direction. Similar allusions to the "elders" occur while the children of Israel were yet in Egypt; but whether these regulations were derived from patriarchal times we have no direct proof. Moses, the founder of the Hebrew Commonwealth, was reared and educated in the palace of Pharaoh, and thereby doubtless possessed the most favorable opportunities for developing his talents. He might, it is proper to assume, have enjoyed the highest honors under the king, had he desired them, as the princess regarded him as her son. But the sight of his suffering brethren filled him with grief and turned his thoughts to devising methods for their relief. He abandoned the splendor and luxury of the palace to lead the life of a simple shepherd in Midian, where he remained for forty years, in the meantime doubtless perfecting plans to secure the release of his enslaved brethren. He married the daughter of Jethro, a priest of the Midianites, and a man of much wisdom, as appears from every allusion to him, and from the excellent advice he gave to Moses. Forty years having elapsed, Moses reappears in Egypt as the deliverer of his people, with his plans and methods all carefully arranged for the accomplishment of his noble purpose. In the narration of the manner of the release, doubtless the real and the figurative are intertwined in accordance with the style of the writers of the ancient East. The release is effected, and the children of Israel, numbering six hundred thousand men capable of bearing arms, which represented, according to the generally accepted estimate, a total population of three millions, march forth from under the thraldom of Pharaoh, and establish their national independence and civil freedom.

Having crossed the Red Sea, the first significant step taken by Moses is the separation of Church and State, by causing the priestly duties to devolve upon Aaron, and the military command upon Joshua, while Moses retains the entire charge of the civil administration, until about the third month of the wanderings, when they arrive at the foot of Mount Sinai. Then "It came to pass on the morrow that Moses sat to judge the people." When Jethro, who had joined Moses, saw how he was occupied in judging between one and the other, he very wisely counselled Moses how to delegate his authority for the greater advantage of his people and with benefit to himself. "The thing that thou doest is not good — this is too heavy for thee; thou art not able to perform it thyself. Moreover, thou shalt provide out of all the people able men, such as fear God, men of truth, hating covetousness, and place such over them to be rulers of thousands and rulers of hundreds, rulers of fifties, and rulers of tens. So Moses hearkened to the voice of his father-in-law, and did all that he had said." — Exodus xviii., 13-24. That he did so hearken and follow this wise counsel of his father-in-law appears by Moses' own statement some forty years afterward, as contained in Deuteronomy i., 9, 13, and 15: "And I spake unto you at that time saying, 'I am not able to bear you myself alone. Take you wise men, and understanding, and known among your tribes, and I will make them rulers over you.' And ye answered me and said, 'The thing which thou hast spoken is good for us to do.'" These and other similar passages distinctly prove the practical establishment and adoption of the essential principles of democratic government. First, that of representation — the text is (*häbü*), take you or select for yourself, not that I will make rulers over you of my own selection; but the words of Moses are: "Take you or select for yourselves," and such as you select I will make them rulers. Secondly, we discover here the recognition and adoption of the principle of civil equality in its fullest application, in that we find that the rulers and officers were not to be taken from any special favored or privileged class, but "out of all the people." And who were these rulers to be? Were they to be men of wealth from any particular tribe or family? No, they must be men of recognized fitness and capacity, of high moral worth, pure and righteous men who would not betray their sacred trust for selfish ends. "Able men, such as fear God, men of truth, hating covetousness — wise men, and understanding, and known among your tribes." These were the qualities that the representative must possess, that are as all-sufficient now as they were then, and of which the American people were continually reminded during the period of their organization of government by the public orators and preachers of election sermons.

The children of Israel having arrived in sight of the Promised Land, their great lawgiver summons them all before him; he recounts to them their whole eventful history, their hardships, their toils, their sufferings and their triumphs; he recapitulates and codifies their laws and causes them to be written in one brief book, the Book of Deuteronomy, which are thereupon adopted by the whole people under the most solemn and awe-inspiring circumstances. He admonishes them to keep these laws fresh in their memory, and directs that they shall be read before all Israel at the end of every seven years, in solemnity of the year of release, on the Feast of Tabernacles. The people bind their part of the covenant by answering: "All that Jehovah hath spoken we will do." Moses then commits the book of the laws into the custody of the Levites, the tribe especially set apart for the service of religion and as instructors and teachers of the nation, who, as Moses expressly declares: "Shall teach

Jacob thy judgements, and Israel thy law." Moses is succeeded by Joshua, who leads his conquering armies over the Jordan. Before settling in the Promised Land the law is again promulgated, and Joshua is confirmed as chief executive by the voice of the people. Joshua is succeeded by the Shophetim or Judges, of whom the Scriptures enumerate fourteen in all, from Othniel to Samuel.

The Judges were elected by the people, and summoned to power as the necessities of the times demanded; they were statesmen-heroes, and after the occasion for which they were called to assume the head of the confederate nation had passed away, they usually retired to their humble occupations, as was notably the case with Gideon. The government under the Judges was very much like our own Federal Government: each tribe had its own tribal or state government, which had jurisdiction over all local affairs, and it sent its duly elected representatives to the national congress. This government, from the fact that God, the source of all power, the embodiment of the law, and not a king, was ruler of the nation, is termed by various writers a Theocracy, or Nomocracy (from *nomos*, meaning law), or a Commonwealth.

Many writers fall into the error of defining this theocratic government as a government by priests, or a purely religious commonwealth. The very fact that the Levites, the tribe of priests, were separated from the other tribes, and that, with the single exception of Eli, no priest was ever elected to the chief magistracy during the entire period of the Commonwealth, decidedly negatives any such interpretation. The central or national government was divided into three departments; they were:

First. — The Chief Executive, who was styled Judge or Shophete.[1] He was vested with chief command in war, and was at the same time the first magistrate in peace. He summoned the senatorial and popular assemblies, proposed subjects for their deliberation, presided in their councils, and executed their resolutions. In the words of the learned Calmet: "He was protector of the law, defender of religion. He was without pomp, without followers, without equipage. The revenue of his office was merely gratuitous. He had no settled stipend, nor did he rise any thing from the people."[2] That the Chief Executive might not wield arbitrary power, and at the same time to divide the responsibility of government and thereby to aid him in conducting the affairs of state, a Senate was elected of seventy elders.

Second. — The Senate, Sanhedrim or Synedrium. Whether it had its origin in Jethro's advice to Moses, above referred to, or came into being a year later (Numbers xi., 16, 24), is a matter concerning which biblical expositors are divided. That a permanent national senate was created at this latter period is maintained very generally by Jewish writers, as well as by such scholars as Sidney, Grotius, and Selden. The former claim that this

---

[1] The Carthaginians had rulers, whom they styled Suffetes, whose name seems to be derived from the same stem, and whose authority resembled in some particulars that of Shophetim, or successors of Joshua. Livii: Hist. Lib., xxviii., 37, Lib. xxx., 7.

[2] See also Lowman on "Civil Government of the Hebrews," ch. 10; and Dupin, "Complete History of the Canon," Bock I., ch. 3, sec. 3.

senate continued with but short interruptions from that time until the Babylonish captivity, and was revived and reorganized on more definite principles after the return of the Jews to Jerusalem. Some writers even go so far as to deny that this council of seventy was a legislative body, and claim that it was purely judicial. I am inclined to the opinion that although its chief functions were legislative, and occupied the same position in the frame of government as our senate, yet it was at the same time a high court of justice, the legislative and judicial departments being united as in the English House of Lords. The learned commentators Michaelis and Jahn agree in their views as to the nature and functions of this senate. I quote the former, who says: "Moses established in the wilderness another institution which has been commonly held to be of a judicial nature, and under the name of Sanhedrim or Synedrium, much spoken of both by Jews and Christians, although it probably was not of long continuance.[1]

"A rebellion that arose among the Israelites distressed Moses exceedingly. In order to lessen the weight of the burden and the responsibilities that oppressed him, he chose from the twelve tribes collectively a council of seventy persons to assist him. It seems much more likely that this selection was intended for a Supreme Senate."

---

[1] J. M. Mathews, D.D., in his book of lectures entitled "The Bible and Civil Government," proves quite conclusively that the senate was a permanent national body. "It seems, in some respects, to have been like an Upper House, as the senate in our own government, or in other respects like a High Court of Appeal, whose decisions and ordinances would give weight to their proceedings and their acts." — P. 227.

Third. — The Assembly. This was the popular branch of government, and that such existed is very evident from numerous passages which directly refer thereto, and from distinctions made between "all Israel" and this third department or assembly. Its characteristics and constitution are not so definitely laid down as those of the senate, nor does the Scriptures inform us of how many individuals it was composed. This assembly is styled generally the "Congregation," the "whole Congregation," "all the Congregation," and that these terms did not mean all the children of Israel numerically, but only in their representative capacity, is clear from the context itself, especially when, from the nature of the occasion, the whole population could not have possibly acted. For instance, when it was commanded respecting an offender, "Let all the congregation stone him," it surely could not have meant that the three million should do it? "From various passages of the Pentateuch," says the learned commentator, Michaelis, "we find that Moses, at making known the laws, had to convene the whole congregation of Israel; and in like manner, in the Book of Joshua, we see that when Diets were held the whole congregation were assembled. If, on such occasions, every individual had to give his vote, every thing would certainly have been democratic in the highest degree; but it is scarcely conceived how, for this circumstance alone must convince anyone that Moses could only have addressed himself to a certain number of persons deputed to represent the rest of the Israelites. Accordingly, in Numbers i., 16, mention is made of such persons, and in contradistinction to the common Israelites they are there denominated Kerüe Häeda — that is, those wont to be called to the convention." Algernon Sidney, whose "Discourses concerning Government" was the chief textbook of the founders of our government, and whose works were to be found in the libraries of Franklin, Adams, Jefferson, and many others of our scholars, statesmen, and divines, sums up his estimate of the Hebrew Commonwealth in these words: "Having seen what government God did not ordain, it may be reasonable to examine the nature of government he did ordain, and we shall find it consisted of those parts, besides the magistrates of the several tribes and cities: They had a chief Magistrate, who was called Judge or Captain, as Joshua, Gideon, and others; a Council of seventy chosen men, and the General Assembly of the people. The first was merely occasional, like to the Dictators of Rome. The second is known by the name of the Great Sanhedrim, which, being instituted by Moses, according to the command of God, continued till they were all, save one, slain by Herod. And the third, which is the Assembly of the people, was so common that none can be ignorant of it, but such as never looked into the Scripture."[1] The author then cites Josephus, Philo, Maimonides, and Abarbanel in confirmation of his text.

Aside from this popular and progressive system of government that was organized by Moses and his immediate successors, a number of statutes were passed, doubtless with a view of raising the people up to such a standard of moral worth that they might be a law unto

---

[1] "Discourses Concerning Government," Chap. II., Sec. 9.

themselves and long cherish the blessings of civil freedom under their God-given government; statutes that lie at the root of our most advanced civilization, that embody the highest justice and the broadest humanity. They had their statutes of limitations, which provided that at the end of every cycle of seven times seven years, in the year of jubilee, all debts should be cancelled and all unfulfilled obligations annulled. In that year, likewise, all agricultural property and all realty other than real estate located in walled cities was to revert to the original owner or to his heirs at law, discharged from all liens, debts, and encumbrances. In this wise the permanent accumulation of large tracts of lands in single hands or families was rendered impossible, and thereby would have been prevented that species of slavery known as the feudal system.

No better law than that of Moses could have been devised to maintain political equality. The effect was the same as if the state retained the fee and every fifty years made leases to every head of a family at a nominal rental. In fact, we find a positive provision that the land should not be permanently alienated: "The land shall not be sold forever; for the land is mine, for ye are strangers and sojourners with me" (Levit. xxv., 23). The homestead and exemption laws find their origin in the following humane provision of the Mosaic code: "No man shall take the upper or neither millstone to pledge; for he taketh a man's life to pledge." The principle embodied in this law is being gradually recognized in the civil laws of all nations, that a man cannot by distraint for debt be deprived of the necessary means of sustaining life. Provisions were also made prohibiting the land proprietor from gleaning the fields and reaping the corners, so that the poor and the stranger might gather the leavings, and thus be relieved without being humiliated.

Akin to his humane and tender consideration for the poor are the statutes requiring the master to pay the hire of his servant promptly on the day when due: "Neither shall the sun go down upon it, for he is poor and setteth his heart upon it." There is a sense of mingled kindness and justice expressed in this injunction, and the reasons assigned for its strict obedience appeal touchingly to the master's obligation. Numerous other laws of universal application are contained in this code, which provides not only for justice tempered with mercy, as between man and man, but prohibits cruelty towards the lower animals.

The lessons of the decline of this republic are as valuable and instructive as that of its development. It was not subverted by force nor by the tricks or cunning devices of unscrupulous leaders, as was the case with the Grecian, Roman, and Venetian republics, but by the people exercising their democratic prerogative, the right of choice to set up over themselves such form of government as they might elect. Their original constitution provided for such a contingency, and while giving warnings against it, contained instructions for establishing a form of monarchy which would be farthest removed from tyranny. Thus we see at this early period of mankind — 1,500 years and more before the Christian era, before Rome had obtained a foothold in history, 500 years before Homer sang, and 1,000 years before Plato had dreamed of his ideal republic, when all Western Europe was an untrodden wilderness — the children of Israel on the banks of the Jordan, who had just emerged from centuries of bondage, not only recognized the guiding principles of civil and religious liberty that "all men are created equal," that God and the law are the only kings, but also established a free commonwealth, a pure democratic-republic under a written constitution, "a government of the people, by the people, and for the people."

CHAPTER VII.

The Influence of the Hebrew Commonwealth Upon the Origin of Republican Government in the United States

It is remarkable, that of the many historians who have written so ably and minutely of the history of the United States, none should have observed in his writings the relationship between our republic and the commonwealth of the Hebrews, especially in the light of the earliest constitutions of several of the New England colonies expressly framed upon the model of the Mosaic code as a guide, and of the frequent references thereto made by the ministers in their political sermons, who constantly drew their civil creed from the history of those times, and held up this ancient form of government as a model inspired under the guidance of the Most High.

The distinguished Jonathan Mayhew, the divine whom Robert Treat Paine styled "the father of civil and religious liberty in Massachusetts and in America," who suggested to James Otis the idea of a committee of correspondence,[1] a measure of great efficiency in producing concert of action between the colonies, and who as early as 1750 delivered a discourse against unlimited submission and non-resistance, a sermon which was characterized as "The morning gun of the Revolution," in a later discourse delivered in Boston on May 23, 1766, on the "Repeal of the Stamp Act," says: "God gave Israel a king (or absolute monarchy) in his anger, because they had not sense and virtue enough to like a free commonwealth, and to have himself for their king, — where the spirit of the Lord is there is liberty, — and if any miserable people on the continent or isles of Europe be driven in their extremity to seek a safe retreat from slavery in some far distant clime — O let them find one in America."

Samuel Langdon, D.D., the President of Harvard College, who, through the influence of John Hancock, was installed in that office as the successor of Samuel Locke, and who, afterwards, in 1788, was a member of the New

---

[1] The General Court of Massachusetts originated the measures that resulted in the union of the colonies by instituting the "Committee of Correspondence," who should keep each colony advised of what was passing in all the others, and should concert plans of action. This idea came from Dr. Mayhew, who wrote to James Otis in 1766 as follows: "Lord's Day, June 8th. To a good man all time is holy enough, and none is too holy to do good, or to think upon it. Cultivating a good understanding and hearty friendship between these colonies appears to me so necessary a part of prudence and good policy that no favorable opportunity for that purpose should be omitted." He then adds: "You have heard of the Communion of Churches: — while I was thinking of this in my bed, the great use and importance of a Communion of Colonies appeared to me in a strong light, which led me immediately to set down these hints and transmit to you."

Hampshire convention when the constitution came before that body for adoption, in his election sermon delivered before the "Honorable Congress of Massachusetts Bay" on the 31st of May, 1775, taking as his text the passage in Isaiah, i., 26, "And I will restore thy judges as at the first," etc., delivered a most eloquent discourse, wherein he traces the history of government from the first recorded beginning, and defines its functions and prerogatives with a logic that proves him to have been well versed in the doctrines of civil liberty as handed down through the writings of Sidney, Milton, Hoadley, and his eminent predecessor, Locke. These are his words: "The Jewish government, according to the original constitution which was divinely established, if considered merely in a civil view, was a perfect republic. And let them who cry up the divine right of kings consider, that the form of government which had a proper claim to a divine establishment was so far from including the idea of a king, that it was a high crime for Israel to ask to be in this respect like other nations, and when they were thus gratified, it was rather as a just punishment for their folly. Every nation, when able and agreed, has a right to set up over itself any form of government which to it may appear most conducive to its common welfare. The civil polity of Israel is doubtless an excellent general model, allowing for some peculiarities; at least, some principal laws and orders of it may be copied in more modern establishments."

By a special vote Dr. Langdon's sermon was ordered to be printed and sent to each minister in the colony and to each member of the Congress. What effect such words as these had upon the minds of the people in general in preparing them for independence, as well as upon the founders of our republic, each and all of whom doubtless read this sermon, is scarcely a matter of conjecture when we take into consideration that he was not only a ripe scholar occupying the most important literary position in America, as President of Harvard College, but one of the foremost ministers and pulpit orators, as well as an acknowledged authority in the science of government.[1]

On the 17th of May, 1776, which was kept as a national fast, George Duffield, the minister of the Third Presbyterian Church in Philadelphia, with John Adams as a listener, drew a parallel between George III. and Pharaoh, and inferred that the same providence of God which had rescued the Israelites from Egyptian bondage intended to free the colonies. The election sermon of the following year was preached on the 29th of May, 1776, some forty days before the Declaration of Independence, before "the Honorable Council and the Honorable House of Representatives of the Colony of Massachusetts Bay," by the Rev. Samuel West. He was not behind his professional brethren in zeal for the welfare and liberty of his country. He was a member of the convention for forming the constitution of Massachusetts, and of that of 1788, which ratified the Constitution of the United States. He took his text from Isaiah i., 26, the same as was taken by Dr. Langdon above quoted. He discusses the entire political situation of the times. "We are to remem-

---

[1] See notes, page 111.

ber that all men being by nature equal, they have a right to make such regulation as they deem necessary for the good of all; that magistrates have no authority but what they derive from the people." He then passes in review those two famous passages from the New Testament, which I have already referred to, under whose authority monarchs, tyrants, and usurpers have claimed as sanctioned by Holy Scriptures the right of obedience under all circumstances, and from which were deduced the doctrines of "Divine Right," and "Unlimited Submission." From this he passes in review the history of civil government, and sums up by saying: "There was great deal of propriety in the advice Jethro gave to Moses to provide able men — men of truth, — and to appoint them for rulers over the people; (then quoting the words of David): 'He that ruleth over men must be just, ruling in the fear of God.' "

The election sermon in 1780 was delivered before the same body, the Council and House of Representatives of the State of Massachusetts, by Rev. Mr. Simeon Howard, who succeeded Dr. Mayhew as pastor of the West Church of Boston. Among his hearers were Robert Treat Paine and Samuel Adams. The latter submitted to Rev. Mr. Howard the resolution of both Houses of the General Assembly, containing an expression of thanks, and requesting a copy for the press. Taking as his text Exodus xviii., 21 — "Thou shalt provide out of all thy people able men, such as fear God, men of truth, hating covetousness; and place such over them to be rulers," he divides his sermon under four heads: 1st. Necessity of civil government; 2d. The right of the people to choose their own rulers; 3d. The business of rulers; and 4th. The qualifications as pointed out in the text as necessary for civil rulers. His sermon is almost entirely devoted to the exposition of the Hebrew Commonwealth under Moses; that it was a government by the people under the guidance of God Almighty; and the rulers were not appointed, but elected. His words are: "This is asserted by Josephus and plainly intimated by Moses in his recapitulatory discourses, and indeed the Jews always exercised the right of choosing their own rulers; even Saul and David and all their successors on the throne were made kings by the voice of the people."

On May 8, 1783, at Hartford, before "His Excellency Governor Trumbull and the Honorable General Assembly of the State of Connecticut," the election sermon was preached by the eminent President of Yale College, Rev. Dr. Ezra Stiles, who as early as 1760 predicted that "the imperial dominion will subvert as it ought in election." He was the lifelong friend of Franklin, and to whom Franklin, who was regarded by some as an atheist, because his pure and simple deism conformed with no established sect, wrote in his eighty-fourth year as follows: "You desire to know something of my religion; it is the first time I have been questioned upon it. Here is my creed: I believe in one God, creator of the universe; that he ought to be worshipped; that the most acceptable service we render to him, is doing good to his other children. As to Jesus of Nazareth, I think his system of morals, as he left them to us, the best the world ever saw, or is like to see; but I apprehend it has received various corrupting changes, and I have some doubt as to his divinity."[1] Dr. Stiles, taking for his text Deut. xxvi., 19 — "And to make thee high above all nations which he has made, in praise, and in name, and in honor," etc., delivered a discourse — subject, "The United States Elevated to Glory and Honor." This sermon takes up one hundred and twenty closely printed pages, and assumes the proportions of a treatise on government from the Hebrew Theocracy down to the then present, showing by illustration and history that the culmination of popular government had been reached in America, transplanted by divine hands in fulfilment of biblical prophecy from the days of Moses to the land of Washington; and discussing from an historical point of view "the reasons rendering it probable that the United States will, by the ordering of Heaven, eventually become this people."

His words are: "Here (at the foot of Mount Nebo) the man of God, Moses, assembled three millions of people — the number of the United States, — recapitulated and gave them a second publication of the sacred Jural Institute, delivered thirty-eight years before under the most awful solemnity at Mt. Sinai. He foresaw indeed their rejection of God, whence Moses and the prophets, by divine direction, interspersed their writings with promises that when the ends of God's moral government should be answered, he would recover and gather them (quoting Deut. xxx., 3) 'from all the nations whither God had scattered them.' Then the words of Moses hitherto

---

[1] See Bigelow's "Life of Franklin, Written by Himself," vol. III., p. 459.

accomplished but in part, will be literally fulfilled. I shall," he continues, "enlarge no further upon the primary sense and literal accomplishment of this and numerous other prophecies respecting both Jews and Gentiles in the latter-day glory of the church; for I have assumed the text only as introductory to a discourse upon the political welfare of God's American Israel, and as allusively prophetic of the future prosperity and splendor of the United States." Referring to the success of our armies under Washington, whereby the independence and sovereignty of the United States was established and recognized by Great Britain herself in less than eight years, he says: "Whereupon Congress put at the head of the spirited army the only man on whom the eyes of all Israel were placed. Posterity, incredulous as they may be, will yet acknowledge that this American Joshua was raised up by God for the great work of leading the armies of this American Joseph (now separated from his brethren), and conducting these people to liberty and independence." Such is the reasoning of Dr. Stiles, a man who was held in the highest esteem and most profound respect by every American for his learning, patriotism, and wisdom. Chancellor Kent said of him, in an address delivered at the Yale Commencement in 1831: "A more constant and devoted friend to the revolution and independence of his country never existed. Take him for all in all, this very man was undoubtedly one of the purest and best-gifted men of his age."

On December 11, 1783, appointed as a day of thanksgiving by Congress, upon the restoration of peace, Rev.

Dr. Duffield, of the Third Presbyterian Church in Philadelphia, and one of the chaplains of Congress, preached the sermon of the day before a most distinguished audience of citizens and legislators. Dr. Duffield was also one of the most eminent divines in America, recognized not only for his great learning and eloquence, but prominent by reason of his zeal in the cause of independence, and for his devotion to the public welfare, and for his commanding influence among his fellow men. This sermon, together with others to which reference has been made, illustrate how thoroughly the pulpit was imbued with the Mosaic ideas and polity. The affairs of the colonies in their every condition were constantly compared with those of the children of Israel. Dr. Stiles, in his celebrated sermon above quoted, went so far in that direction as to advance reasons why the aboriginal Americans were none others but the lost tribes of Israel, and that therefore the same Providence guided their destiny. Dr. Duffield, referring to the causes which led to the American revolution, that it was brought about by reason of the British monarch's determination to reduce the colonies into absolute vassalage, carries forward the analogy in these words: "Some have ascribed this extravagant conduct to the same spirit of jealousy which once influenced the councils of Egypt against the house of Joseph, lest waxing too powerful they might break off their connection, and pursue a separate interest of their own." He calls attention to the providential success that crowned the American cause, that in eight short but eventful years the thirteen dependent colonies had become thirteen independent States. He explains how these wonderful results were brought about in a summing up that consists of a climax of Mosaic analogies: " 'Tis He, the Sovereign Disposer of all events, hath wrought for us, and brought the whole to pass. It was He who led his Israel of old, by the pillar of fire and the cloud, through their wilderness journey, wherein they also had their wanderings. 'Twas He who raised a Joshua to lead the tribes of Israel in the field of battle; raised and formed a Washington to lead on the troops of his chosen States. 'Twas He who in Barak's day spread the spirit of war in every breast to shake off the Canaanitish yoke, and inspired thy inhabitants, O America! It was He who raised up Cyrus to break the Assyrian force, and say: 'Let Israel be free'; endued the monarch of France with an angel's mind, to assert and secure the freedom of his United American States. And He alone who saith to the proud waves of the sea: 'Hitherto shall ye come, but no farther.' "

These constant references, parallels, and analogies to the children of Israel in their struggle for political liberty would not have been made again and again if they did not meet with a responsive echo in the minds and sentiments of the large audiences to whom they were addressed throughout the thirteen colonies. A volume would not contain all the politico-theological discourses delivered during the decade prior to the restoration of peace, wherein the Hebrew Commonwealth was held up as a model, and its history as a guide for the American people in their mighty struggle for the blessings of civil and religious liberty. I have purposely only quoted such of these discourses as were delivered by ministers who were eminent not only in the pulpit, but were equally distinguished as scholars, as patriots, and as legislators.

Thus far the Hebrew Commonwealth has been referred to as the model and guide adopted in the sermons and discourses of our patriotic divines; we shall now trace it in the halls of legislation, and in the writings and political pamphlets published during the period prior to the adoption of the Constitution. We must not lose sight of the fact that neither the Declaration of Independence nor the success of our armies in the struggle decided for us our form of government, or secured for posterity the blessings of civil and religious liberty, — the former only served to make the latter possible. These were the victories of the statesmen, the heroes, and of the patriots of the pen. The machinery of government under the articles of confederation was so defective, weak, and ineffectual that men, wise men, true and loyal Americans, aye, many in the army, by reason of the inability of the government to pay the half-starved soldiers, demanded a government that would revive from prostration the public credit and faith of the nation, that would provide for the payment of interest on the public debt; they felt the need of a government with a strong arm, an elective monarchy. "Now, just as day was dawning and independence about to be secured, every thing seems to tumble in chaos about them, threatening a state of things worse than their former condition as colonists."[1]

---

[1] See article in *Harper's Magazine*, Oct., 1883, by J.T. Headley.

A paper embodying the views of the army of Washington while stationed about Newburg was drawn up and presented to their commander-in-chief by Colonel Nicola, an old army officer, held in high esteem by Washington. This, after describing the perilous state of feeling in the army and the dangerous aspect of affairs, and showing the necessity, now that peace was assured, of settling at once on a form of government which should be a strong one, took up the several forms of government in the world, and summed up by declaring that a republican government was the most unstable and insecure, and a constitutional monarchy like that of England, the strongest and safest, and, in short, offered to make Washington dictator. It concluded by saying: "Owing to the prejudices of the people it might not at first be prudent to assume the title of Royalty, but if all other things were adjusted, we believe strong arguments might be produced for admitting the title of King." Like Gideon, the righteous judge of the Hebrew Commonwealth, whom the people of Israel offered to make king in their unbounded gratitude, and in admiration of his signal service in delivering them from the hands of their most powerful enemies, Washington declined the crown.

This monarchical-party spirit was so strong, that it survived even after the adoption of the Constitution until the election of Jefferson as President, who refers to it in his inaugural address.[1] No one arraigned the monar-

---

[1] Jefferson writes as follows in the introduction to his "Anas": "The contests of that day were contests of principle between the advocates of republican and those of kingly government." See also letter of James Monroe (Dec.,

chical tendencies with a more vigorous and fearless pen; no one contributed more in keeping alive the fires of liberty during those times that tried men's souls, than Thomas Paine, that much maligned and abused man, who has been accused of every crime that malice could invent. Paine was the friend of Franklin, though whose patronage he came to America; he was the editor of the *Pennsylvania Magazine*, the Secretary of the Committee of Foreign Affairs of the Continental Congress; he was beloved and esteemed by Washington, by whom he was invited, when in distressed circumstances, to share the hospitalities of his home, to whom James Monroe, in 1794, then Minister to Great Britain, wrote, while Paine was confined in the Luxemburg as prisoner, by the order of Robespierre, for espousing the cause of liberty in France, as follows: "You are considered by them (the people of the United States) as not only having rendered important services in our own revolution, but as being on a more extensive scale the friend of human rights, and a distinguished and able advocate in favor of public liberty. To the welfare of Thomas Paine the Americans are not, nor can they be, indifferent." Washington says of the author of "Common Sense," in a letter to Joseph Reed,

---

1816) to Andrew Jackson, giving his recollections of the monarchical tendencies which were shown by certain leaders of the Federal party, both before and after the adoption of the Constitution. He says: "Many of the circumstances on which my opinion is founded, took place in debate and in society, and therefore find no place in any public document. I am satisfied, however, that sufficient proof exists, founded on facts and opinions of distinguished individuals, which became public, to justify that which I had formed...."

dated January 31, 1776: "A few more of such flaming arguments as were exhibited at Falmouth and Norfolk, added to the sound doctrine and unanswerable reason contained in the pamphlet 'Common Sense,' will not leave numbers at a loss to decide on the propriety of separation." "This book" ("Common Sense"), says Dr. Rush, "burst forth from the press with an effect that has been rarely produced by types and paper in any age or country." The former part of this remarkable production is devoted to the subject of "Monarchy and Hereditary Succession." The argument is drawn entirely from the Hebrew Commonwealth. "Monarchy is ranked in Scripture," says he, "as one of the sins of the Jews, for which a curse in reserve is denounced against them." "All anti-monarchical parts of Scripture, have been very smoothly glossed over in monarchical governments, but they undoubtedly merit the attention of countries which have their governments yet to form." And then he recites the history of the entire "transaction," to the introduction of Saul as King. "But where, say some," are his words, "is the king of America? I'll tell you, friend: he reigns above, and doth not make havoc of mankind like the royal brute of Britain. Yet that we may not appear to be defective even in earthly honors, let a day be set apart for proclaiming the charter; let it be brought forth placed on the divine law, the word of God; let a crown be placed thereon, by which the world may know that, so far as we approve of monarchy, in America the law is king."

He narrates the conduct of that truly great judge of Israel, who was summoned by the voice of the people from the wheat field to assume the chief magistracy of the nation, and to deliver his people from their strongest and most powerful foes, the Midianites. These are his words, in the second chapter of "Common Sense": "The Jews, elated with success, and attributing it to the generalship of Gideon, proposed making him king, saying: 'Rule thou over us, thou and thy son and thy son's son.' Here was temptation in its fullest extent; but Gideon, in the piety of his soul, replied: 'I will not rule over you, neither shall my son rule over you; the Lord shall rule over you.' Gideon doth not decline the honor, but denieth the right to give it." Paine then continues the scriptural narrative concerning the people demanding the king, about one hundred years after this period, under Samuel, and quoting in full Samuel's admonitions, concludes in these words: "These portions of the Scripture are direct and positive; they admit of no equivocal construction. That the Almighty hath here entered his protest against monarchical government is true, or the Scriptures are false."

Unfortunately, we have in most instances only skeleton reports of proceedings and debates of the Federal and State conventions on the adoption of the Constitution. Doubtless the model of the ancient commonwealth, its history and lessons, were frequently employed by the distinguished representatives; the meagreness of the records leaves this to conjecture only. In the Legislatures of the various States before whom the Constitution came for adoption, the delegates again and again referred to this original model of popular government. In New York, for instance, Robert R. Livingston, the chancellor of the

State, refers to it[1]; so also John Lansing,[2] who, in his speech urging its adoption, says: "Sir, the instances from the history of the Jewish Theocracy evince that there are certain situations in communities which will unavoidably lead to results similar to those we experience. The Israelites were unsuccessful in war; they were sometimes defeated by their enemies. Instead of reflecting that these calamities were occasioned by their sins, they sought relief in the appointment of a king, in imitation of their neighbors." So also the Hon. Mr. John Smith,[3] who quotes in full the admonition of Samuel to the children of Israel, describing the manner in which a king would rule over them. In short, again and again, in and out of our halls of legislation, was the history of the Hebrew Commonwealth referred to, narrated, rehearsed, and analogies drawn therefrom by the advocates of a republican form of government in answer to those who favored monarchy, so that the admonitions of Samuel were as familiar to the people of America as the words of the Lord's Prayer.

In the light of these facts it is not at all surprising that the committee, which was appointed on the same day the Declaration of Independence was adopted, consisting of Dr. Franklin, Mr. Adams, and Mr. Jefferson, to prepare a device for a seal for the United States, should, as they did, have proposed as such device, Pharaoh siting in an open chariot, a crown on his head and a sword in his hand,

---

[1] Elliot's Debates, Vol. II., page 210.
[2] Elliot's Debates, Vol. II., page 218.
[3] Elliot's Debates, Vol. II., pages 225 and 226.

passing through the dividing waters of the Red Sea in pursuit of the Israelites; with rays from a pillar of fire beaming on Moses, who is represented as standing on the shore extending his hand over the sea, causes it to overwhelm Pharaoh; and underneath, the motto: "Rebellion to tyrants is obedience to God."[1]

Dr. David Tappan, who, after the declaration of peace, was chosen professor at Harvard College, in the course of his lectures on the "Jewish Antiquities," says that the demand of the children of Israel to Samuel, to set a king over them, was exceedingly displeasing to Samuel, and when he referred the matter to God, the Most High declared that by this act they had rejected him; that he should not reign over them. "From hence some writers have inferred that monarchy is in its very nature criminal; that it impiously invades the prerogative of the Supreme Ruler, as well as the equal rights of man." "This inference," says the learned professor, "was plausibly enforced on the American people, in the beginning of the year 1776, by a very popular but desultory writer (doubtless meaning Thomas Paine), and this sentiment, with others equally well timed, operated, with the swiftness and force of the electric fluid, in preparing the country for a formal separation from the British monarch."

Many more authorities can be adduced upon the same subject, but they would only be cumulative. Through more than a century and a half the Puritan ministers

---

[1] A copy of the report recommending the above device is preserved among the papers of the Continental Congress in the State Department in Washington. For Lossing's design of the seal, see frontispiece.

never tired of dwelling upon the trials, sufferings, and fortitude of the children of Israel during their long and weary wanderings from the land of their oppressors until the organization of popular government on the banks of the Jordan. To what extent these teachings and preachings served as an inspiring incentive to the American people in their heroic struggle for civil and religious liberty, and to what degree the oft-quoted warnings of the last Judge of Israel, followed by the corroborating revelations of scriptural history, supplied the argument that battered down the enslaving doctrine of "Divine Right of Kings," and its corollaries, "Unlimited Submission," and "Non-Resistance," we leave for the reader to draw his own conclusion.

We neither claim nor wish to be understood as inferring that the structural parts of our form of government were derived from what was believed to be the components of the Hebrew Commonwealth, but only that this scriptural model of government, which was democratic, as distinguished from kingly rule, had a deep influence upon the founders of our government and prepared the minds of the people, especially in the New England colonies, so that they not only longed for, but would not content themselves with any other form of government than *that* form which had the divine sanction, the government of the Hebrews under the Judges.

Looking backward over a period of nearly three hundred years it may be difficult for us in this age to understand why the early Puritans should have gone back nearly three thousand years for their form of government, but we must not forget the intense religious spirit of Puritanism, which was a Protestant renaissance of the Old Testament and a reversion to biblical precedents for the regulation of the minutest details of daily life. They were not content even to administer justice by the civil or the common law, but regulated the punishment of crimes by the Pentateuch, and in framing their criminal code every section cited the biblical chapter and verse.

In the study of the history of the development of our form of government, to leave out of account the ecclesiastical side, freedom from Lords-bishop as well as from Lords-temporal, is to overlook not only important but essential elements. In the resolution which led to the first meeting of the Continental Congress, passed by the House of Representatives of Massachusetts Bay on June 17, 1774, appointing Samuel and John Adams, Thomas Cushing, Robert Treat Paine, and James Bowdoin a committee to meet delegates and representatives from the other colonies at a congress to be held in Philadelphia the following September, the reasons recited for such action were "to deliberate and determine upon wise and proper measures, to be by them recommended to all the Colonies for the Recovery and Establishment of their Just Rights and Liberties Civil and Religious."[1] In devising the plan of our government, the founders not only drew their inspiration from first sources but reverted to first principles, the "unalienable rights" of man. They builded well on a broad and lasting foundation, and to

---

[1] MSS, resolution signed by Samuel Adams, clerk, in possession of the author.

their wisdom and foresight we owe the blessings of liberty we enjoy. Freedom of person, freedom of conscience, and a republican form of government, constitute the creed of our political faith, and they alone can insure for us and our posterity liberty, happiness, and stability.

NOTES.

Page 55. For ten years after the settlement of the Bay Colony, the clergy and their followers stubbornly refused to recognize the common law or to enact a code, and when at length, in 1641 further resistance to the demands of the freemen was impossible, the Rev. Nathaniel Ward drew up "The Body of Liberties," which contained a criminal code copied almost verbatim from the Pentateuch. The Pentateuch was also enacted as a whole when the express laws did not cover the case. — "Mass. Hist. Collection," 3d Series, VIII., 216.

Page 77. In this outline of the Hebrew Commonwealth we are chiefly guided by the belief and views of the early founders of our government, who were little troubled by critical doubts; it is their interpretations which concern us here.

Page 94. See Election Sermon by Dr. Langdon delivered at Concord before the General Court, June 5, 1788, entitled, "The Republic of the Israelites an Example to the American States." To which the eminent divine attached a note, that soon after this sermon was delivered the Convention of the State of New Hampshire met (June 21st) and adopted the United States Constitution, thus making the requisite two-thirds, the number of States necessary of its adoption. P. 33.

INDEX.

Adams, C.F, note by, 63
Adams, John, inaugural address of, 7; account of Otis, 21; defense of rioters, 27; quoted, 42, 63, 69-70; member of committee, 44
Adams, Samuel, president of the committee, 31
American colonies prior to the Revolution, 1; monarchical character of, 2; outline of governments of, 3; Congress of, 6; address to king in 1774, 13; desire for republic of slow growth, 22
American colonists, class of, 35
American compact, paper on, 17
Aristotle, quoted, 64

Baird, Robert, quoted, 48
Baltimore, Lord, proprietor of Maryland, 39
Barré espouses American cause, 22
Bernard, Governor of Mass., 26; memorial to the king, 26
Bishops, dread of, in America, 43; restored to House of Lords, 73
Bossuet and Louis XIV., 71
Boston, British troops sent to, 26; massacre in, 26-27; Port Bill passed, 31, reception of, in Boston, 31; tea party, 28; Port Bill, 28, 31; *Evening Post*, quoted, 31-32; alarmed concerning episcopacy, 29-30

Boucher, Jonathan, on Anglican Church, 42-43; on Non-resistance, 74
British troops sent to Boston, 26
Calmet, quoted, 83
Camden, Lord, espouses American cause, 22
Canadian boundaries, 24, 29
Carthage not a pure democracy, 64
Catholic Church, property of, 29
Chamberlain's address on Adams, 47
Charles I., execution of, 72
Charles II., 72
Chatham, Lord, quoted, 70
Christianity, establishment, 67; hindrance to civil liberty, 67
Church of England in Virginia, 40
Church and State, under Charles I., 35; in Virginia and New England, 46-47, 70; union dissolved, 49
Civil liberty did not originate in Greece, 77
Coddington, Gov. of Rhode Island, 39
Colonies all true to respective founders, 19
Committee of Correspondence, 92
Congress of colonial delegates, 6; resolution of, in '76, 7
Connecticut and Mass., last colonies to grant religious liberty, 49
Connecticut, Congregationalists in, 49
Constitution of U.S. and religion, 52
Conway espouses American cause, 22
Cromwell, Oliver, 37
Cushing, 44
Deberdt, agent for Mass., 44
Declaration of Independence, 8-11, 18

Delaware Assembly in 1775, 6
Dickinson, 5, 6
Divine Right of kings, 70, 74; sanctioned by Bible, 70; sanctioned by Church, 72; and unlimited submission, 75
Duffield, Geo., sermons of, 94, 99
East India Company, 27
Election sermons in New England, 58, 91
Encroachments of king, resisted, 75
England, Protestantism in, 68
English and American revolutions, 9
English afraid of Parliament, 62; commonwealth a failure, 61-62; a commercial nation, 25
Episcopalians in America, 73, 74
Established Church, assaults on, 47-48; plan of, in colonies, 49

Europe, disturbances in, 53
Faneuil Hall, meeting in, 31
Filmer, Sir Robert, 72, 75
Foord, John, quoted, 38
Franklin, Ben., agent for Penna., 23
Franklin, gov. of New Jersey, 5
Gage, General, Gov. of Mass., 29
General Assembly, 26
General congress, proposition for, 31
Genesis of the republic, 53
George III., 14, 19, 74, 76, 94
Georgia, Methodists in, 50
Gladstone, quoted, 68-69
Governments of colonies—provincial, proprietary, and charter, 3
Grahame, Hist. of U.S., quoted, 41

Greek and Roman republics, 77
Grenville introduces Stamp Act, 22
Grotius, 83
Hancock, John, 28, 44, 92
Hawley, Major, 44
Hebrews and Puritans, resemblance between, 53-54
Hebrew Commonwealth and United States, 78, 91, not purely religious, 82, 83; council of, 84, 86; congregation, 85; republic, decline of, 88, liberty of, 89
Henry VIII., motives of, 68
Henry, Patrick, against the parsons, 46; speech of, 47
Hobbes, 75
Holland, pilgrims in, 34; precarious state of, 63
Howard, Simeon, sermon of, 95

Hutchinson, Gov. of Mass., 27; refuses to dismiss troops, 27
Inglis, Charles, 45
Israelites, organization of, 78; departure from Egypt, 79
Jahn, 84
James I., reign of transition, 34; absolutism of, 71
Jamestown, 40
Jefferson, Thomas, 18, 31, 42, 48, 50, 102
Jethro, advice to Moses, 79
Jewish antiquities, 107
Judges of Israel, 82
Kings, right of, in the various colonies, 4; divine right of, 13; prayers for, to be omitted, 11
Knowledge, lack of diffusion of, in colonies, 58
Langdon, Samuel, sermon of, 92
Lansing, John, quoted, 106

Laud, 33, 35
Lecky, quoted, 15
Liberty in Virginia and Mass., 47
Livingston, Robt. R., quoted 105
Locke, John, 37, 75
Locke, Samuel, 92
Maryland, Assembly in 1775, 6; Catholics in, 50
Massachusetts, Assembly in, 26, 44; religious intolerance in, 40; Congress thanks ministers, 59
Mather, Cotton, sermon of, 56
Mathews, J.M., quoted, 84
Maury, payment to, test case, 46
Mayhew, Jonathan, sermon of, 57; quoted, 73, 91-92
Michaelis, quoted, 84, 85
Milton, John, 37
Molasses Act, 20, 27

Monarchy and the Church, 67
Monroe, James, quoted, 102
Montesquieu, opinion of republics, 17, 62
Mosaic Laws, adopted in New England, 55; unfitness for, New England, 55
Moses, education of, 78; government of, 80-81
Motley, J.L., quoted, 68
New England, ministers of, interest in politics, 56; Bible in, 53; Confederation, 54
New Jersey, Assembly of, 5; Protestants in, 49
Newport, 39
New Testament, influence of, 14
New York, Church of England in, 49-50; *Gazette*, 17; Provincial Congress in 1775, 6
Nicola, Col., paper by, 102

Non-resistance, doctrine of, 73
North Carolina, religious sects in, 50
North, Lord, moves Boston Port Bill, 31
Novia Scotia, boundaries of, 24
Old Testament, influence of, 14
Otis, James, 21, 45, 92
Paine Robert T., 91
Paine, Thomas, 103
Palfrey, Hist. of New Eng., quoted, 35
Parliament, encroachments of, 25; acts by, 28-29; reasons for favoring Catholics, 29-30; attitude towards Canada, 29-30; consideration of tea riots, 30
Pennsylvania, Assembly in 1775, 5; Quakers in, 50
Philadelphia, meeting in, 28
Pitkin, History of U.S., quoted, 20, 54

Pitt espouses American cause, 22
Political development, 12
Political Register, cartoon in, 45
Pope, power of the, 67
Portsmouth, 39
Presbyterians favored revolution, 47
Price, Dr., 12, 24
Protestant majority in America, 52
Protestantism in England, 68
Providence, 38
Puritans and Pilgrims, difference between, 33-34
Puritans, preference for Old Testament, 54
Quebec Act, 29
Quincy, Josiah, 27
Randolph, John, 18
Religious causes of the Revolution, 33
Religious liberty in Maryland and Rhode Island, 39-40

Republic not favored by colonies, 60-61; of U.S., heir to Hebrew Commonwealth, 107-108
Republics, defects of ancient and modern, 61
Revolutions in different lands, 11; political causes of, 17
Rhode Island, troubles in, 26; government imitation of the Jews, 39; Baptists in, 49
Rush, Dr., quoted, 104
Russell, Lord William, 72
Sanhedrim, 83-84
Sects in different colonies, 49-50
Selden, 83
Sherlock, Bishop of London, 46, 47
Sidney, Algernon, Discourses on Government, 37, 77, 83, 86
Smith, John, quoted, 106
Society for Propagating the Gospel, 45

South Carolina, sects in, 50
Stamp Act, 4, 22, 25, 92
Stiles, Ezra, quoted, 33, 96
Story, Judge, 50
Sugar Act, 27
Superstition in politics, 60-61
Tappan, David, quoted, 107
"Taxation without Representation," first uttered, 21
Taxation, resolutions against, 27-28
Tax on Tea, 25-26, 27-28
Thatcher, Oxenbridge, 21
Theocracy in New England, 54
Tories, 4, 31, 72
Tudor, William, quoted, 45
U.S. Treaty with Tripoli, 52
U.S. Republic planned on Hebrew model, 59-60

U.S. seal, device for, 106-107
Vane, Henry, 37
Virginia, appeal to Parliament in 1764, 4; convention, resolutions of, in '76, 10, resolutions of, in 1774, 31; religious intolerance in, 40-41; Anglicans absolute in, 42; loyalty of, 42; compulsory baptism in, 46; affairs in, 46-47; Dissenters in, 48; Cavaliers in, 50
Warren, Joseph, 31
Washington, quoted, 103-104
West, Samuel, sermon of, 94
Winthrop, leader of Puritans, 33
Winthrop, Robt. C., centennial oration of, 7
Whigs, 4, 31
William III., absolutism of, 13; retrogression of, 13

Williams, Roger, 36-37

www.ingramcontent.com/pod-product-compliance
Lightning Source LLC
Chambersburg PA
CBHW031252290426
44109CB00012B/541